THE MOUNTAIN OF IGNORANCE

SUNDAY ADELAJA

Sunday Adelaja
THE MOUNTAIN OF IGNORANCE
©2017 Sunday Adelaja
ISBN 978-1-908040-38-1

Copyright © Golden Pen Limited
Milton Keynes, United Kingdom. All rights reserved
www.goldenpenpublishing.com

Cover design by Alexander Bondaruk
Interior design by Olena Kotelnykova

WHAT PEOPLE ARE SAYING ABOUT THE BOOK

It takes only a man of deep understanding and wisdom to write this book – Mountain of Ignorance. Pastor Sunday Adelaja is a man who knows how things should be done and when things should be done per moment, no wonder he can birth this particular book.

This book is a manual that must be passed down from this generation to coming ones. It exposes the rottenness in each individual, the body of Christ and our societies today. We must not permit the passing down of this rottenness to the coming generation.

It will take a humble heart to actually read this book to the end because it reveals so much, I mean so much detailed ignorance we operate with, thinking we are on the right path, and making God Himself to be unable to help us, how tragic!

After reading this book you will realize that to every problem we face as an individual or as a nation, there is a particular knowledge missing and the faster we get this knowledge and apply it the faster our problems will get resolved.

The mountain of Ignorance will open your eyes to how much power God has placed in our hands to rule the earth for Him. You will begin to understand that it is our responsibility to build our nations. We are to use our minds as reasoning humans to solve problems.

At the end of reading this book, part of the conclusion you will make is, no one gets to a stage of knowing it all, we all must continue to learn and improve ourselves till the day we die. Living is also learning!

Thank you Pastor Sunday Adelaja, for this book is a bright light to our world.

Dr. Fisayo Ayeye

When I was called upon to write a review about this book, I jumped at it. I immediately concluded that it should be recommended to everyone in a leadership position. If you know what to do, then your Nation will grow. This book will give you the insights needed to solve the most difficult problem in your country.

I will also recommend this book to every young person out there who is passionate about changing their world. After reading this book, I noticed that people are looking up to God for answers when the answer is right in front of them. Ignorance is what makes countries go to war, it is what makes valuable relationships fail, it is what makes people poor. It is what makes countries with God-given resources to still be referred to as an under-developed economy.

Ignorance indeed is a mountain that must be subdued by all. Three basic things that I will always remember from this book:

1. Ignorance is a cancer and you know how deadly cancer is.
2. "Pursue knowledge as though it's your lifeblood then you will know greatness!" Monique Rockliff
3. The quality of your life is directly proportional to the quality of your knowledge.

Dr. Sunday Adelaja is about to reform nations with his new book.

It is a must read for all.

Abidemi Somoye
Author, Economist & Financial Planner
Founder and President, Personal
Finance Tips With Toyin

What a revolutionary book this is! I am so excited to know that an answer to the decadency in our nation and the present day church is being addressed.

The Mountain of Ignorance is surely a must have for everyone, especially those who are tired of seeing the plague of ignorance destroy our people, nation and especially the body of Christ, THE CHURCH!

This book directly hits the nail on the head of the problem we are having in our society today. Truly as this book has rightly stated, what is destroying us today is not satan or our enemies. What is destroying us is ignorance!

Pastor Sunday Adelaja has done another mind blowing job putting this amazing piece of work together that will liberate not just our nation or continent but the world at large. The truth in this book will bring light to every area of darkness and understanding to everyone who will read and put the principles in this book to work.

Thank you sir for this great work you have done for the body of Christ and the world at large. Thank you for your boldness to challenge the ills of our society today.

God bless you greatly!
Dr. Bien Suffient
#1 Bestselling author of
"The Beauty of Challenges"
President @ Kingdom Lifestyle Movement (KLM).

First would like to congratulate my Mentor reformer for passionately putting together such a revolutionary writing against ignorance.

You did an exceptional job in dissecting and exposing ignorance like no book ever written on the subject. It became clear that this is not just another one of your best well researched topics, but your core calling hinges on eradicating ignorance in all its forms; from personal to Church to national.

The book has dug deep into the root cause(the tap root system) of all the problems and evils of society. I think it's became pivotal to address the mountain of ignorance, before tapping into the solutions of our world problems, particularly in our beloved continent of Africa. It is a powerful prelude or required read for any one passionate like the author, anyone who desires to deal with the lofty, dark problems of our nations.

The book is a must read for anyone who has been asking a question; how will the vision 'let there be light' be accomplished in Africa. Here in this book, the hungry are provided with a concrete strategy of how to go about bringing light to this world. It is through knowledge(connotes light) that there will be marked progress, growth and development in our individual lives, nations, continent and the world at large.

So, hence I think this book is loaded with relevant and significant knowledge to enlighten those who read it, that they too can be the light in the darkness around them. No longer would people perish, grope in the dark whilst armed with a book that will serve as a 'switch on' button, to the end of their detrimental ignorance or darkness. The knowledge or light in the book is freely given to illuminate the minds and the paths of the readers to their life of significance.

When trying to compare this book to others; I pondered on how mountains stand high and elevated in the earth, so it is with this book. It stands alone, lofty as the high problem of ignorance that is discussed. In my opinion, it expresses and exposes how the author(and God!) abhors ignorance. The author through this intense writing resolved to be an advocate against ignorance; raising together with him an army that will move all mountains of ignorance in our Church and society.

The Mountain of Ignorance book, like I submitted, is a mountain-moving(moving the stronghold of ignorance that has self-destructed many lives) and an enlightening read. Enlightening in that it sheds some much needed light on the dark problem of ignorance. The desired outcome of reading a book like this is that it should leave readers with a personal responsibility, no longer blaming anyone(not even the devil) for their failures, unhappiness, poverty, unfulfillment... No one to blame even for all the dark problems in our society. But to go for knowledge as if their lives depend on it. The wide spectrum of ignorance has been meticulously explained; no one exempted.

So the call is for everyone who reads, to deal with the mountain of ignorance in front of them. The biggest cry was sandwiched in the middle of the book, to the Church, the pulpit, the nation and the light of the world. That the Church may seriously consider how it has spread ignorance, repent (change mindset and message) to truly be the God-appointed powerful light that is empowered to chase darkness in our world. We have been shown, how in this book. By the power of knowledge!

What a relevant and timely message for Africa and the Church, connecting well with the Author's mission to transform Africa! The more reason I think "Mountain of Ignorance is a must read for those who desire to see their nations transformed. Hence I would like(kindly allow me) to subtitle it; " The power of knowledge in national transformation" because that is how I see it's impact.

Thank you once again for pouring out your soul into this magnificent piece of writing. Kindly receive my first 'big picture' impressions, not that I have apprehended, still well on my way reaching out to my great Light. I am grateful for the opportunity which comes with much responsibility to shine my light. I trust that I have answered to your expectation or even satisfaction. I thank you.

By Nosipho Baloyi
South Africa

TABLE OF CONTENT

PROLOGUE

Dear readers,

Before you start reading this book, I will really recommend to you this prologue because in this tragic story you will see a full illustration of the subject matter of this book. After this book has being written, and ready to be sent to the publisher, I came across a story that was published by 'Abiyamo' which perfectly exemplifies the topic of this book 'The Mountain of Ignorance'. This story like no other illustrates to us why Nigerians, Africans, and Christians, in general, must rise against this huge mountain of ignorance in our country. Ignorance has become a huge mountain that has now seem to us insurmountable, but until we overcome it, dismantle it, and level it, our nation will never be set free from backwardness, darkness, destruction, and economic disaster. This change must start from the church and the believers, here is why.

The city of Ibadan in Oyo State, southwestern Nigeria is one of the biggest in West Africa. It is home to the first college in Nigeria, University of Ibadan, set up by the provincial bosses in 1948. A stand amongst the most well-known elements of this incredible stronghold of learning is its Zoological Garden, which is one of the most established in the nation. The zoo plays host to different creatures however the most incredible of all of them are the lions. For some guests, an outing to the well-known zoo is not finished without seeing the lofty lions. So it was amid the Easter Lenten season of

1991, all of Ibadan was humming with the energy of the season and normally, one of the prime spots of fascination for some families was the University of Ibadan Zoo. Families, couples, and visitors trooped into the zoo that decisive day. Notwithstanding, obscure to the greater part of alternate guests, there was one specific guest who had another plan. Religious activist (some say he was a minister others say he was a church goer) "Daniel" Abodunrin's aim that critical day was not to see the lions and bring some impressive pictures with him. His objective was to show something that had never been accomplished. His arrangement was to reproduce what was recorded in the Holy Bible many years prior to that time. It was the tale of a Jewish boy named Daniel who was caught by King Nebuchadnezzar of Babylon who served in the lord's court until the season of Cyrus, the Persian sovereign.

Quick forward to 1991, area: Ibadan. A minister tried to reproduce what was described in the 6th chapter of the Book of Daniel. Minister Abodunrin wore a long red robe and grasped his huge Holy Bible. As he advanced for the lion walled in area, frightened zoo attendants yelled and cautioned him (some different records expressed that he sneaked in and everything happened quickly while another narration had it that he figured out how to persuaded the zoo managers to permit him to enter and let God exhibit signs and wonders saying that the God of Daniel is the same yesterday, today and tomorrow).

One thing was clear: Abodunrin did not listen to any of those who warned him. He was simply droning Bible verses as loud as possible and talking in tongues. He made it into the walled in area of the lions and gazed at them.

The lions gazed back at him. It was a most discomforting sight for everybody, including the lions. A trade of death gazes and at a point, a stunning hush fell over the entire spot. It was all like a motion picture. Sincere Christians in the group were holding up to see a confidence boosting supernatural occurrence while a few others toughened their brains for the bloodiest dramatization of the century. Driven by the energy and enthusiasm of religion and with the most extreme conviction that he would be spared by the Holy Spirit or that the heavenly attendants will deaden the lions as they accomplished for Daniel, Abodunrin did not quit droning Bible verses and talking in tongues, wriggling his body under the robes, giving what was the scene of the year for everybody in the zoo. A group had assembled. Be that as it may, inside the den of the lions, something fascinating was going ahead with the Nigerian Daniel and the catlike brutes.

As Abodunrin drew nearer them, the enormous felines withdrew and moved towards an edge of their confine, that was their nature. They pulled back from the advancing 'man of God'. Right then and there, everybody was viewing the whole dramatization as though it was a fantasy. Here was a man in a streaming red robe, equipped with only an expansive Bible, drawing nearer a portion of the fiercest animals on earth.

At the point when Abodunrin bounced into the lions' den, the lions moved into a strained retreat. Abodunrin ventured closer. He resolved to turn the daring animals into goats. He felt he had all the magnificent power and profound forces to summon holy messengers to tame the lions. The best way to deaden a lion in a moment is to utilize a sedative dart, which is simply judgment skills.

Be that as it may, the prophet felt things in the physical world are controlled in the domain of the spirits and there was no requirement for any sedative dart, he would utilize his Bible as a narcotic for the lions.

He got over the individuals who cautioned him, saying that they had a fleshly sense of judgment and couldn't comprehend things of the spirit. The crowd were looking like they were watching a gala concert.

He may have mixed up the retreat of the lions for an indication of shortcoming or that the heavenly attendants were really working their marvels as of now. Like an agitated personality, Abodunrin continued droning Bible verses, making signals at the lions and commanding them to stay composed. He was approaching the God of Daniel who spared the prophet in Babylon to indicate marvelous force.

As he made the last approach towards the lions, what happened next was a blaze, the lions lifted their enormous bodies and charged at Abodunrin. A sharp battle followed and the scared group couldn't trust the scene before their eyes. It appeared everybody was excessively confounded, making it impossible to try and do anything. Minister Abodunrin couldn't believe his eyes and as the lions arrived on him, the look of dread in his eyes must be better envisioned. In a matter of seconds, he was torn to shreds. He passed on the spot and the lions nibbled on his remaining parts. Abodunrin's red robe was redder with the splatter of his blood everywhere and his torn bloodied Bible lie in one corner of the lions' den.

Today, numerous evangelists over the globe have made endeavors to reproduce the described stories and supernatural occurrences of the Bible yet they have finished sadly, from the minister who drowned while attempting to stroll on water to another minister who entered a lion's den in Taiwan just to be injured subsequent to yelling to the lions: 'Jesus would spare me!'.

Nigerians need to figure out how to be levelheaded rather than living in ignorance of religious philosophies.

INTRODUCTION

Dear friends!

Our generation is a blessed one. We are so blessed to be among the living in this season. I count it a great privilege from God.

Our society today is vast with different technologies, scientific theories, applied sciences, cybernetics, different types of equipment, computers, electronics, the Internet etc. Science has gotten to its peak of development in comparison to the generations past. Information can be gotten at the tip of our fingers. It is called THE AGE OF INFORMATION.

Yet sadly, Ignorance seems to be the number one disease plaguing our society today. It is disheartening that so many people still suffer from this dangerous plague called IGNORANCE. Irrespective of the fact that information can be readily gotten in every sphere of life today, ignorance has become a mountain in our society and world at large. The Mountain of Ignorance has become a stumbling block to the advancement of most people in our generation.

The worst case scenario is with the vast majority of people that are ignorant and do not even recognize it. This indeed is the most demolished state any man can be in.

It is one thing to be sick and you know that you are sick; it is another thing to be totally sick without you knowing. The lack of knowledge of your state will prevent you from going to the doctor to look for help. This, in fact, is one of the major causes of death from some cases that might have been treatable if noticed on time.

For instance, if cancer is discovered in its early stage, in most cases, it can be treated, but if discovered late, then it leads to death. The same case that was treatable in one person will now be leading to death in another person. What is the reason for death in this case? Nothing but IGNORANCE!

Ignorance in my opinion, is the most deadly cancer plaguing our world today. The fact that you did not know you had cancer is not going to stop the cancer in your body from killing you. "I did not know" in this case is not an excuse; neither is it going to change anything. That is why we are often advised to go for a general checkup from time to time in other to have a full knowledge of the state of our health. You don't have to wait till when you have symptoms of a disease to do these checkups, neither do you have to wait till when you can't get up from your bed anymore. Hence it is always expedient to carry out regular check up with your doctor, even though you are not sick.

In the same way, it is advisable to always learn and seek to get new knowledge in every aspect of life. Irrespective of your profession, educational background or qualifications. Age should never be a limiting factor in gaining new Knowledge. Your talents should not be a stumbling block.

Knowledge is always progressive. In order for you not to be caught up in the web of this dangerous plague, you have to always make a continuous and conscious effort to learn.

"Those people who develop the ability to continuously acquire new and better forms of knowledge that they can apply to their work and to their lives will be the movers and shakers in our society for the indefinite future." (Brian Tracy)

This book, therefore, will serve as a checkup for everyone, even those who think they are free from the deadly cancer called IGNORANCE.

My loving readers, the fact that you are reading this book right now is a proof that you are on the move to pull down this plague, this cancer, THE MOUNTAIN OF IGNORANCE.

Keep reading! I believe this book is not just going to serve as a checkup but will offer the necessary treatment needed to heal this deadly plaque, irrespective of its stage in our lives, church and society at large.

Let The Journey Begin!

Sunday Adelaja

PART 1

PERVASIVENESS OF IGNORANCE

CHAPTER 1
....

KNOWLEDGE IS LIGHT, IGNORANCE IS DARKNESS

"The light of knowledge is fully capable of destroying the darkness of ignorance. This also helps us in overcoming all the difficulties and in achieving success in all our endeavors"
(Sam Veda)

There is no greater wealth one can have than knowledge. Knowledge is the foundation for every success in life. Knowledge they say is power. The difference between the rich and the poor is knowledge. The difference between successful people and failures is knowledge. The difference between those who live a fulfilled life and those who are unfulfilled in life is knowledge. Knowledge indeed is power!

Without knowledge, it is impossible to operate at your maximum capacity in life. For you to be relevant in our world today, you must be knowledgeable. The true beauty of life can only be revealed through knowledge and its application. The main weakness of a man is in the area of his ignorance. You are at a great disadvantage when you lack knowledge. Life is not always fair to the ignorant; life will serve you according to your level of knowledge. In some cases, even though you are rich without knowledge which is very rare, you might not be able to enjoy it.

Mary was a poor widow who lived in Los Angeles in the 1970s. She could barely make ends meet, as she struggled to feed herself and her daughter. She was living in an old two-roomed apartment with her daughter, Victoria. Mary became sick and was admitted to the hospital. The doctor told her she needed to carry out a heart surgery urgently, in other to save her life. The surgery was to cost 4500 USD, which she could not afford and as a result, she lost her life leaving her only daughter behind.

Six months after her death, some bankers traced her to her house to deliver to her what her parents left behind for her, only to discover that she was dead. They found the daughter and informed her that her mother had 20million USD to her name. They told her that her late grandparents left the money for her mum before her death, as she lost her both parents when she was only 10yrs old. Victoria was asked to sign some papers and the money was transferred to her. She could not hold her emotions as she wept helplessly, knowing that her mum died for lack of 4500 USD, even though she was a millionaire, 20 million dollars rich.

This woman lived and died in abject poverty because of ignorance. There is no telling how disadvantaged we are when we lack knowledge. You might be reading this story and in your mind you are saying, what a sad story! But how many more things do we miss out in life due to ignorance? How many opportunities do we lose to ignorance on a daily basis? How many friends and relationships have we lost because of ignorance? Surely you can never live a comfortable and fulfilled life without knowledge.

This is basically the number one problem we have in

Nigeria and Africa as a whole. Ignorance is plaguing our nation and continent. We need to pursue knowledge and put importance on knowledge so we can move our nations and continent forward.

WHAT THEN IS KNOWLEDGE

Knowledge can be defined as:

• Acquaintance with facts, truths, or principles, as from study or investigation; general erudition: knowledge of many things.

• Familiarity or conversance, as with a particular subject or branch of learning: knowledge of accounting was necessary for the job.

• Acquaintance or familiarity gained by sight, experience, or report: knowledge of human nature.

• The fact or state of knowing; the perception of fact or truth; clear and certain mental apprehension.

• Awareness, as of a fact or circumstance: he had knowledge of her good fortune.

• Something that is or may be known; information: he sought knowledge of her activities.

• The body of truths or facts accumulated in the course of time.

From the above definitions, I believe we now have a broader view of what knowledge is. The beautiful thing about knowledge is that you can get it any time you want. It is one of the cheapest, yet most powerful assets at our disposal. Bless God for the globalization; there is hardly any topic you seek knowledge in that you will not find on the internet. You can decide to be knowledgeable; it is not something someone dictates for you. You do not need to take permission from anyone to get knowledge. This precious gift is inexpensive and free in most cases. All you need to achieve this is through determination, discipline and hard work.

No one was born knowledgeable but as we grow up, it is our duty and total responsibility to acquire knowledge if we must live a good, happy and successful life. Hence leaving ignorance behind; which could be said to be a childhood trait. This simply means the acquisition and love for knowledge is a sign of maturity. In other words, I can say it's not a crime to be ignorant as a child, but I think it is a great crime to self and others to remain ignorant as an adult. In the words of Apostle Paul to the Corinthians:

When I was a child, I talked like a child; I thought like a child, I reasoned like a child. When I became a man, I put the ways of childhood behind me.

1 Corinthians 13:11

From the scripture above, I can see that the different transitions in the life of Paul the Apostle occurred as a result of acquiring knowledge, which he did consciously. Getting knowledge or eradicating ignorance needs a conscious effort. It is our individual responsibility to seek knowledge as we grow up in our everyday life. It will therefore not be wrong to say, being ignorant is a sign of immaturity (childishness), while been knowledgeable is a sign of maturity (adulthood). Knowledge is the only force that can pull down ignorance. THE MOUNTAIN

OF IGNORANCE! It is necessary and expedient to seek knowledge in every area of our life. This is the only way you can live a happy and fulfilled life, and not become a danger to yourself and others.

KNOWLEDGE IS LIGHT

"Knowledge once gained casts a light beyond its own immediate boundaries" (John Tyndall)

Knowledge is the light that shines in our minds and causes creativity, development, civilization, organization, etc. The world has gone through the different evolutional phases to what we have today, thanks to knowledge. From the Stone Age to the modern age, the only major difference is the progression of knowledge, **"not that we now lack stones"**.

Knowledge is, therefore, the answer to our everyday question. We sometimes call the Stone Age the Dark Age which simply means that ignorance is actually darkness; hence without any doubt knowledge for sure is light. The same word used for light in Greek, is also used for knowledge (τὸ φῶς "The light" is from phos, which means both "light" and is the metaphor for "knowledge"). Knowledge is the only power that drives away ignorance; just in the same way as light drives away darkness. In order to pull down THE MOUNTAIN OF IGNORANCE in our society, we must imbibe knowledge in ourselves and our society.

For us to have a civil and civilized society today, we must embrace knowledge. Knowledge should be a possession everybody should eagerly pursue to have. It is only knowledge that can set a person, society, nation, continent and world free from destructive practices. The solution to our every problem is hidden in knowledge, the very light that shines and overpowers darkness (ignorance).

"Someone once remarked that while ignorance was the curse of God, knowledge was the important power of wings which carried one to heaven". A famous Sanskrit verse says that an educated person is honored everywhere. The importance of a knowledgeable person is immense. Where-ever he goes, he is offered a place of reverence, a scat of authority, and he commands the hearing of everyone present. The power of knowledge lends him such distinction.

KNOWLEDGE IS POWER

Knowledge is the foundation for a successful life. You are what you know. The quality of your life is directly proportional to the quality of your knowledge. You can never live better than what you know. Who you are today, the kind of life you live, whether you are fulfilled or unfulfilled, satisfied or unsatisfied are a direct reflection of what you know. Hence the popular saying KNOWLEDGE IS POWER!

The power of Knowledge is the power of transformation. There can't be any transformation without knowledge. Knowledge can be said to be the very integral, fundamental, essential, basic, intrinsic part of life. Its importance in life is second to none. It is vital that we take the issue of knowledge acquisition seriously.

"Pursue knowledge as though it is your life-blood, then you will know greatness!"
(Monique Rockliffe)

For you to be great in life you have to be in constant pursuit of knowledge. Knowledge is the only thing that distinguishes the wise from the foolish. It is thanks to knowledge that we can say we have the elites in our societies today. The only difference between where you are and where you want to be is knowledge. You will always be limited in life, if your knowledge is limited. So enlarge your coast of knowledge!

Knowledge is a powerful and a very important part of Life that should never be underestimated. Knowledge is a powerful acquisition in life which when given to someone does not decrease. It is knowledge that has equipped man with the limitless power with which man dominates over all living things which are physically much stronger than him. Knowledge has significantly helped him to conquer nature; this conquest has prompted human progress and civilization. It is thanks to knowledge that we have many scientific, medical and geographical discoveries. Many people have become scientists. They have invented many scientific apparatus.

Doctors and scientists have contributed a lot to the service of humanity. Doctors have the knowledge of various organs of the body. Many deadly diseases have become curable. A lot of research work is still going on in the field of medical science to improve the health of people.

Geographical discoveries have made the world a small place. Man acquired the knowledge of directions and then began their journey to discover new places. Sea routes were discovered between Asia and Europe. A person who studies history acquires the knowledge of the events of the past. We get information about ancient people, society and kingdoms. Knowledge of history gives us the opportunity to learn from the mistakes of the past, and to avoid it in the future.

Knowledge brings power to life. Those who have knowledge are capable of leadership, they rule the world. But the power that comes from knowledge gives meaning, progress to life. It enables solutions to the problems of mankind. It eradicates ignorance and illuminates darkness in the life of humans. Knowledge plays an important role in life. Knowledge is an asset that should be pursued and acquired by every living soul.

I hope that all human beings will come to the understanding of the power and importance of knowledge in life. It is only knowledge that can promote our zest for life. Sadly though, so many people are indifferent to knowledge today. They don't pursue it; neither do they seem to know the significance and importance of it. They pay little or no attention to this very important factor of life, knowledge! Hence the domination of ignorance in our societies today, which has resulted in different problems: disasters and catastrophes, we have in our lives, societies, nations, continent and world at large.

It is the apathy to knowledge that led to the rule of ignorance which created a difference in humanity and nations. Have you ever wondered why some people are fulfilled and others are not? Have you ever wondered why some are in lack and hunger, while others have so much to eat and live in surplus? Well the answer is not far-fetched, KNOWLEDGE!

- The difference between a developed nation and a third world nation is knowledge.
- Knowledge is the difference between a civil and uncivil society.
- Knowledge is the difference between a poor nation and a wealthy nation.
- Knowledge is the difference between the poor and the rich.
- Knowledge is the difference between the strong and the weak.
- Knowledge is the difference between success and failure.
- Knowledge is the difference between the depressed and the cheerful.
- Knowledge is the difference between the literate and illiterate.
- Knowledge is the difference between the godly and ungodly.
- KNOWLEDGE IS EVERYTHING.

> *"Knowledge is in every country the surest basis of public happiness."*
> *(George Washington)*

The reason why over half percent of the world is poor today is lack of knowledge. I know a lot of people think it's about geographical location. Some think it is because of their family background. I hear people say, "I didn't have the opportunity to go to school because my family was not rich that is why I am struggling today. If only

I had the kind of privilege or opportunity Mr. A has, I would have been very rich". But that is not true, it is totally irrelevant.

In actual sense of it, poverty or riches, having a fulfilled or unfulfilled life is not a function of ethnicity, race, geographical location, nationality, color of skin, mother tongue, family background, parents, relatives, "nobody to help me" etc. It is rather a direct function of knowledge. You can be anything you want to be in life if you have knowledge. You can't be richer than your level of knowledge. Even if you do, let say you were fortunate and your parents transferred their possessions to you. If you don't acquire knowledge on how to manage the riches (possessions), and how to multiply it, it will just be a matter of time and you will go back to square one. The money or riches will develop wings.

Dear readers, I hope that you will agree with me now that the quality of your life is directly proportional to the quality of your knowledge. Having established that fact, it will now be easier for us to see why knowledge is light in the real sense of it. Light gives us a sense of direction in darkness. We cannot see or walk in the dark but the moment light comes on, there comes a sense of direction.

The same thing with knowledge, if you lack knowledge, you will not be able to work effectively. Even though your two eyes are wide open, you will not be able to see opportunities. You are blinded to the various opportunities for greatness and self-development that comes your way because you lack knowledge. Let's all therefore continuously make the pursuit of knowledge our priority. For knowledge is light! Knowledge is power!

IGNORANCE IS DARKNESS

Ignorance is a serious challenge in our society today. So many people pay little or no attention to the issue of ignorance in our society. Most issues we have in the society are a result of ignorance. Ignorance is a serious cloud of darkness that hovers over a city. As a matter of fact, there is no evil in the society that cannot be traced back to ignorance.

The same word used in Greek for ignorance is also the word used for darkness (τῇ σκοτίᾳ, "Darkness" is skotia, which means both "darkness" and is the metaphor for "ignorance."). Living a life of ignorance is like living in a dark house. Can you imagine yourself living in a totally dark house for a whole day, without any blink of light? I bet that day is going to be very miserable. Yet that is what we do when we live a life of ignorance. In this case is not even just for a day but many years and in most instances, for a whole life time.

Wow! Can you begin to imagine how ineffective you will be for that whole day living in a totally dark house? You will not be able to cook or eat, you will not be able to shower and you will not be able to move freely without hitting an object. You are not going to be able to do anything at all. That whole day is going to be fruitless and useless to you.

From this illustration you will understand better now, why most people live a very fruitless and useless life, year in year out. It is a clear case of living in ignorance. Living a meaningless life, a life of ignorance is the sole reason for all the problems in our society. To put an end to living a meanings life, a life of ignorance (darkness), we have to embrace knowledge (light). We have to turn on the light in that house in order for darkness to give way. It is only knowledge that can pull down ignorance. Let us therefore equip ourselves with knowledge so as to pull down THE MOUNTAIN OF IGNORANCE.

It is a fact that no one was born with knowledge. But let it be known to you that every mind was created with the capacity for development. Hence it is every individual's responsibility to acquire knowledge. It is a sin to the mind to live in ignorance. Ignorance is darkness and as such should be eradicated from the life of everyone.

> *"Every mind was made for growth, for knowledge, and its nature is sinned against when it is doomed to ignorance."*
> *(William Ellery Channing)*

No one was created by God to live in ignorance. We all need to grow and embrace knowledge. We need to develop ourselves on a daily basis in order to have a fulfilled and meaningful life. We cannot afford to settle for anything less. We are made for the best. We are God's creation, created in His image and as such must strive to be like Him. We must dominate the earth through knowledge and proffer solution to the common problems of man and its environment.

God entrusted the earth in our care to manage. Without knowledge, we can't fulfill our responsibility towards God. We were made for the top, created to be the best of all God's creation. We can't afford to live like animals by living in ignorance. We have to make friends with knowledge. We have to seek for it more than a choice silver or gold.

Receive my instruction, and not silver; And knowledge rather than choice gold.

Proverb 8:10

Ignorance is indeed darkness and Knowledge is light. Let us therefore take a decision today and make a conscious effort to acquire Knowledge. The darkness in Nigeria and the African continent today, is ignorance. This is the reason why our nation and continent is backward. We need to bring the light of knowledge to our nation and continent. This message should be what will preoccupy our churches, mosque, schools, social groups etc. NGOs should be created to create awareness and teach people the value of knowledge and the light that comes with it.

LET THE REVIVAL AND THIRST FOR KNOWLEDGE BEGIN!!!

NUGGETS
FROM CHAPTER 1

1. Knowledge is light.
2. Ignorance is darkness.
3. Knowledge is the foundation of a successful life.
4. The difference between a developed nation and an undeveloped nation is knowledge.
5. The difference between the poor and the rich is knowledge.
6. The quality of life is not based on geographical location but on knowledge.
7. The quality of life is not based on ethnicity, race, nationality or even school education but on knowledge.
8. The mind was created with the capacity to develop.
9. It is our individual responsibility to acquire knowledge.
10. It is a wrong to self and others to live in ignorance.

CHAPTER 2

·······················

WHY MOUNTAIN OF IGNORANCE?

"The only thing worse than human igno-rance, is human pride in that ignorance."
(George Takei)

I like you to just travel with me for a few seconds into a world of imagination. Just try to imagine if all our roads, I mean every road on the earth were high moun-tains. Try to visualize how movement and transporta-tion would have been like. Would it have been very easy to move from one point to the other or to travel from one place to the other? Of course the answer is no. For a better understanding of the topic at hand; I like us to take a brief look at what a mountain is.

WHAT IS A MOUNTAIN?

According to the Oxford English Dictionary a moun-tain is defined as "a natural elevation of the earth surface rising more or less abruptly from the surrounding level and attaining an altitude which, relatively to the adjacent elevation, is impressive or notable." From Wikipedia; A mountain is a large landform that stretches above the surrounding land in a limited area, usually in the form of a peak. A mountain is generally steeper than a hill. Mountains are formed through tectonic forces or volca-nism. These forces can locally raise the surface of the earth. Mountains erode slowly through the action of rivers, weather conditions, and glaciers. A few mountains are isolated summits, but most occur in huge mountain ranges.

From the definitions above, you could see that mountains are the highest elevated points on earth. A mountain could have been a great obstruction if there were to be no way around it; owing to the tedious nature or work it takes to climb it. Thank God there are ways around it, if not, not everybody would have been able to climb to get over to the next destination. Looking at how obstructive mountains can be, the impossibility of seeing through it, how it will prevent you from seeing ahead (seeing what is on the other side of the mountain); it will then be clear to you the limiting force ignorance holds on the society. It will further give you a better and vivid understanding of what ignorance can do to our individual lives and that of our nation, if a radical action is not taken against it. **This is the very reason why this book is called The Mountain of Ignorance.**

Therefore using mountain as a parallel for ignorance, I believe will help us to understand the predicaments and the weight of the issue at hand, the issue of IGNORANCE! We need to know the great need and urgency in our topic of discussion today in relation to our purpose and effectiveness as God will have us be on earth.

Ignorance has become like an exalted mountain in the body of Christ today especially in Africa, in our society and the world at-large. It has been decorated in such a way that it seems very beautiful, strong and like a norm or standard of doing things. Most of the clichés people live by today are born out of ignorance. Ignorance indeed has become like a mountain in our society today. If nothing is done and done fast about it, it is going to lead to the total destruction of the church, society and the world at large.

The same way we have seen from our description of mountains above that mountains are domineering in nature. So is ignorance! There is nothing more domineering in our society today than ignorance. Ignorance is the greatest limitation in the development of our society. Ignorance is the number one obstruction to personal development. Ignorance is the sole reason for poverty in our society today. Ignorance is the reason for poor living standards. Ignorance in most cases is the reason for premature death. Ignorance is the reason for all national and international wars. Ignorance is the reason for all economic failures. Ignorance is the foundation for every problem we have in the society today. Ignorance is indeed domineering. Yes Ignorance is a negative dominating force in operation in our various societies today and as such must be pulled down!

My dear reader, God has set you and I here on planet earth for a time as this, and we are going to do something about it. The mountain of ignorance must be pulled down in the body of Christ, in our society, in our nations and in the world at large. It might look as though it is a difficult mission but with knowledge, determination, unity, patience and faith, the mountain of ignorance will be made plain.

What is even scarier about ignorance is the fact that it possesses a strong deceptive nature. Most times ignorant people are not even aware of the fact that they are ignorant. Ignorant people are the most assertive, bold and "all knowing". They are the ones that are not ready to take any correction or listen to the opinion of others. They are quick to see the wrongs and mistakes of others yet are very blind to theirs. They are most often sure of how right they are on all issues without a second thought. Ignorant people are not thoughtful in taking decisions, drawing conclusions on situations and on people.

A perfect example is the case of Mr. James who was a successful business man. He had a friend, Mr. Peter, who was also a successful business man but deals majorly in real estate. Mr. James was offered an opportunity to invest in real estate business, which looked very catchy and lucrative from its prospectus. He knew very little about real estate business. When he told his friend about it, who had more knowledge and experience in that area, he advised him against it, that it was not a good deal. When he discovered that Peter called the company to make inquiries about the business deal he became very furious, concluding that Mr. Peter was trying to "double cross" him in the business proposal. Even though Mr. Peter was calling on his behalf, he refused to listen to him or allowing him to explain the reason why he had to call the company.

Mr. James hurriedly went to accept the business proposal, took a loan from the bank and invested in it, in order to stop Peter from "outsmarting him". After which he cut ties with his friend Peter. Well in conclusion, within three months the business failed just as Peter had said. He became bankrupt, lost his home and his friend.

I am sure most of us can relate to this story. I wonder how many times some of us have assertively accused people of things they never did out of ignorance, even to our own detriment. When we are so assertive of things we do not understand or have little knowledge of, we often end up on the wrong side of life. Ignorance indeed has a destructive force embedded in it.

For any nation or people to come to civilization, they must embrace knowledge. Yes for sure the mountain of ignorance must be leveled from our society, nation, world and most especially the body of Christ.

LIGHT IS MEANT TO SHINE

I see ignorance in the Church as the worst thing that can happen to any society. Do you want to ask me why? Oh yes! The church is the very institution created by God to address the issue of ignorance in the society and bring light (knowledge) to every area of darkness (ignorance). But if the Church fails in her responsibility and now lives in ignorance, WHAT THEN IS THE HOPE OF THE SOCIETY?

Ye we are the light of the world. A city that is set on a hill cannot be hid.

Mathew 5:14

The church is the light of the world. In the scripture above Jesus clearly made it plain to us that we are the light of the world and that we are made to shine. Just as a city that is set on the hill cannot be hidden, so are we supposed to be outstanding in shining our light. But today the church is hidden in the four walls. We are not shining our light; hence darkness has overtaken our society. It is high time we take responsibility for the ills caused by ignorance in our society.

Ignorance has taken an upper hand in the society today, because the church that was meant to eradicate ignorance is also living in ignorance. The church has become comfortable in ignorance. Ignorance is ravaging our world, because the church allowed it to be so. It is time we come together to raise war against this mountain. It is time we put all our efforts together, with a common purpose of leveling the mountain of Ignorance in our nations and world at large.

Almost every problem we see in our homes, churches, societies, nations and the world at large today are all as a result of ignorance. There are hardly any challenges, problems, catastrophes you can mention exiting in our world today that has no connection or root with ignorance. So you can see that really, ignorance has been a mountain! And we have to pull it down as a matter of urgency.

Dear readers, to make my point clear, I would like us to take a look at some of the major problems we have around us today in our society and make an attempt to find the root cause. There is hardly any problem or evil that has no connection with Ignorance. I believe this exercise will help us to understand better why we need to put an end to the plague of ignorance in our world as fast as possible.

I would like you to be very open minded to this exercise, and then you will understand and come to the conclusion of this same truth that Ignorance is the root cause of all the problems, troubles, ills and evil in existence. It will always enlighten us on how we can perfectly provide solutions to these problems by dealing with it from the root cause. Instead of being so concerned about solving its effect. It is easy to provide a permanent solution when you know the cause of the problem

For example if someone is suffering from brain tumor and as such he or she has constant headache which is just a symptom. If because they have a headache and you begin to give them all kinds of pain killers to stop the pain, then you actually have not helped the person. You are actually making his/her case worse, even though there might be a temporal relief of the pain at the moment. Until you get to the root cause of the headache which is the brain tumor, you cannot provide a lasting solution to the problem; you will just be treating the symptom. That is what we do in real life most times, we are more concerned about symptoms. We are so carried away seeking to provide solution to the symptoms that we forget about the root cause of the problem that led to the symptoms in the first place. This is what this exercise will help us correct.

LIST OF SOME SOCIETAL PROBLEMS:

- Poverty
- War
- Illiteracy (poor or no value for education)
- Murder/Suicide/Abortion
- Terrorism
- Racism
- Environmental Pollution
- Global Warming
- Sexual Perversions
- Political Correctness

- Unemployment
- Bankruptcy
- Divorce
- Materialism
- Obesity/Diseases etc.

POVERTY

Let's take look at the issue of Poverty. A lot of people feel that poverty has to do with location, the country you are born in, where you live, the home you were born into, whether your family is rich or not. But the truth of the matter is, the list above, has little or nothing to do with most of the poor people living in our world today. The number one cause of poverty is financial ignorance. It does not matter how much you give to someone who is ignorant financially, sooner or later he will return to his original poverty state. Researches have shown that majority of the people that win the lottery soon become bankrupt after a period of time.

According to a 2010 study by researchers at Vanderbilt University, the University of Kentucky and the University of Pittsburgh, the more money you win the lottery, the more likely you are to end up bankrupt.

The authors divided past lottery winners into two separate groups: those who had won cash prizes between $50,000 and $150,000, and those who had won $10,000 or less. What they found is that those who had won the more sizable sums were more likely to have filed for bankruptcy five years later. Similar research from the National Endowment for Financial Education estimates that 70 percent of people who had unexpectedly come into large sums of money ended up broke within seven years.

This is to show that in most instances the poor needs are not financial gifts (money), but financial knowledge. If financial donations or gifts were a solution to the problem of poverty, then most of the third world nations today should no longer be having issues of poverty; as they have received millions upon millions of financial aid from the western and first world countries. You will agree with me that those financial aids have provided little or no help to the economy of the nations that received it.

WAR

The only reason for war is ignorance; be it national or international war, There is no justification for war; neither is war a perfect solution to any problem. Wars always leave more casualties, and cause more destruction than the problem or misunderstanding that lead to the war. I see war as one of the greatest acts of ignorance in action. You might want to argue, "Oh no, that's not true, some wars are an act of national defense on part of one of the nations involved". As factual as that may seems, if it was not as a result of an act of ignorance, from the other country, there won't be any need for defense.

It is only ignorance that causes one nation to suppress and control the other. It is only ignorance that makes one human being feel that he is better than another, or that his life is more valuable than the other. Where there is knowledge, there would be a sense of humanity among humans, and every life will be valuable. Equality will be the order of the day. It takes KNOWLEDGE TO LIVE

IN PEACE - living in peace with one another as individual, as a nation, as a continent and as a world.

On 28 June 1914, a Serbian shot an Austrian. Within six weeks, many of the countries of Europe had become involved in a war that was to cause the deaths of 10 million soldiers, but was the assassination the only cause of war? The assassination of Archduke Franz Ferdinand signaled the rapid slide into world war, but this wasn't the only cause. There were underlying causes in the run-up to the First World War.

In the 1930s, historians argued that there were four underlying long-term causes of the First World War:

Nationalism - the belief that your country is better than others. This made nations assertive and aggressive.

Imperialism - the desire to conquer colonies, especially in Africa. This brought the powers into conflict - Germany wanted an empire. France and Britain already had empires.

Militarism (Arms Race) - the attempt to build up a strong army and navy gave nations the means and will to make war.

Alliances - in 1882, Germany, Austria-Hungary and Italy formed the Triple Alliance. This alarmed, France, Britain and Russia. By 1907, they had all joined the Triple Entente. Europe was divided into two armed camps, to help each other if there was a war.

As much as all these four causes of war might be facts no doubt, but the root cause of it all is ignorance. We all know how destructive wars have been to us as individuals, nations, continents and world at large. For us to be able to live in peace and bring a permanent solution to the problem of war, we must deal with it from the root. Ignorance has to be eradicated and replaced by knowledge. The knowledge of the value of every human life has to be taught and made a priority in our different societies before the placement of personal or national interest. It is only through knowledge prioritization by our nations that we can level THE MOUNTAIN OF IGNORANCE and put an end to war or reduce it to the nearest minimum.

ILLITERACY (POOR OR NO VALUE FOR EDUCATION)

The only reason for illiteracy and poor attitude to education is ignorance. This will in turn reflect on the nation's economy and the general living condition of its citizens. To put an end to this, we must sensitize the masses on the need for education. When I am talking about education, I am not just referring to getting a degree, even though that is very important. What I will rather want to emphasis here is being educated in different spheres of life.

So many people are illiterates when it comes to financial management, investments, entrepreneurship, computer operation, social media etc. We have to deal with this issue of ignorance by knowledge, encouraging people to embrace education. The masses need to know that education is progressive throughout their life time.

MURDER/SUICIDE/ABORTION

Why will another human choose to terminate the life of another human being or terminate his/her own life if not for ignorance? The lack of knowledge of the value and price of life is what pushes people into putting an end to life.

Murder: so many people commit murder today out of hatred, envy, jealousy; the belief that someone else is the reason for their failure or lack of success in life. All these are attributes of ignorance. If we were to be knowledgeable, we would know that our success or failure in life totally depends on us. It has little or nothing to do with someone else. If everyone had the knowledge of their self-value and internal ability to be successful, then there won't be any need for hatred, envy and jealousy towards our fellow humans.

We have to come to the realization that, we as humans have need for each other. The knowledge of the power of good relationship with others is one of the greatest attribute to success. This knowledge will help us to learn from those that are ahead of us, instead of being envious of them, having hatred for them, or seeing them as an obstruction to our success. We have to know that there is enough space on earth for everyone to shine and be successful. No one can stop you from being successful. The only person that can stop you is you. In the real sense of it, you don't need the position of another person to be successful, create your own. You don't need to kill another person to get to your desired height. Rather work hard for it and you will even attain a higher height honorably.

So many religious killings (murder) going on in our world today. This is another level of ignorance. Any religion that will encourage you to terminate the life of another is not a religion that is worthy of your followership. Knowledge will help us to live and tolerate each other irrespective of our religions, beliefs or faith.

<u>Suicide:</u> It is ignorance that leads to frustration and depression, to the point of a person taking his/her own life just to escape from life challenges. Bitterness and emptiness are direct products of ignorance. Knowledge of the purpose and value of life will help an individual to live a fulfilled life, irrespective of the struggles of life. The knowledge of the value of life eradicates the ill feelings we have about the uncertainties and challenges in life. It saves us from the ignorance of terminating our own lives as a solution to our problems.

<u>Abortion:</u> If murder is defined as killing of one human being by another, then abortion is murder. It is ignorant to claim that abortion is not murder, when it is clearly the termination of the life of another human, irrespective of any claims. If you and I were terminated during pregnancy, I do not think we would be in existence today. It is therefore ignorant and a high level of inhumanity to legalize abortion. There is no justifiable reason for the willful termination of the life of another human, in this case, an innocent child.

TERRORISM

Terrorism has become a dangerous plague in our society today. Ignorance led to the rise of terrorism. It is ignorant to think that you can use violence to bring a permanent solution to a problem or to think that by instilling fear into people through terrorism, you become supreme. The ignorant quest for power and supremacy has led to the subjugation of other human beings through terrorism.

Religious terrorism is the most deadly and devastating form of terrorism in operation in the 21st century. It is ignorant to believe that every other human who does not have the same belief or religion as you do should be killed in order to make your religion supreme. It is ignorant to think that killing is a service to some god whatsoever.

It is total ignorance and manipulation in the highest order, to brain wash people into believing that committing suicide (suicide bombers) to kill non-believers of your religion is martyrdom. It is high time we awaken to the reality staring us in the face; it is high time we kick out ignorance and embrace knowledge. Ignorance has done more harm to our society than any other evil you can think of.

RACISM

Racism is an inhumane act that comes from ignorance and greed. Greed on its own is also a product of ignorance. Racism began in the 16th and 17th century as a result of the slave trade. The Europeans and the western world didn't become slave traders because they were racist; they became racist because they enslave the people of color, which occurred through slave trade. The foundation and number one purpose of slavery was economically based. This led to the act of enslaving people of color and dominating them, in order to use them for their profit, and for the betterment of their economy and advancement of their nations.

I can therefore make bold to say that greed is a product of ignorance led to slave trade, and the enslaving of humans (people of the black race), and the inhumane treatment given to them led to racism. So the same factor of ignorance is responsible for racism. It is only ignorance that institutes a person's mindset to think that he is better than another; or that his life is of more value than that of others. Ignorance leads to oppression, subjugation and segregation. Ignorance is the number one problem in our society to today. For us to put an end to all the evils in our society, we must embrace knowledge and eradicate ignorance. The mountain of ignorance must be made plain!

The same thing is applicable to every other societal problem. It is amazing that most times we do not connect the problems in the society with the question of ignorance. The earlier we do this the better and easier it will be for us to resolve the different problems we have in our different societies and our world at large.

> "There is no evil in the universe which is not the result of ignorance, and which would not, if we were ready and willing to learn its lesson, lead us to a higher wisdom, and then vanish away."
> (James Allen)

It is clear that we can put an end to ignorance in every sector and fabric of our society. This simply means if we tackle this Mountain of Ignorance, we would have gotten a solution to almost all the problems we have in our society. All we have to do is to bring light into every area dominated by ignorance in our society. Scriptures continually use these terms, "light and darkness," as metaphors for knowledge and ignorance. Knowledge is light; ignorance is darkness. So in every area of darkness (ignorance) we bring in light (knowledge) and that settles it, for darkness has no power over light. Darkness disappears in the presence of light. God is light! The devil is darkness. When we bring light/knowledge (God) to every sphere of the society, we can be rest assured that every darkness/ignorance (devil) disappears.

Dear brothers and sisters if we have faith, we can say to the mountain of ignorance, "be removed" and it will be removed. This means, it's not enough to have faith but we have to act, we have to say (work) to bring it to pass.

He replied, "Because you have so little faith. Truly I tell you, if you have faith as small as a mustard seed, you can say to this mountain, 'Move from here to there,' and it will move. Nothing will be impossible for you.

Mathew 17:20

If ignorance is equivalent to darkness as seen above then all hope is not lost yet, for darkness has no power over light. We are the light of the world and as long as we are ready to shine our light, darkness will have no resting place anymore to dwell in our society. For knowledge naturally drives out ignorance! We need to step out of our comfort zones and shine our lights, seek for knowledge and put an end to APATHY TOWARD KNOWLEDGE.

"Nothing in the world is more dangerous than sincere ignorance and conscientious stupidity."
(Martin Luther King Jr.)

I believe you will agree with me now that ignorance is really dominant in our society; its negative effect is evident in our world today. Having mentioned that ignorance is equivalent to darkness and knowledge is equiv-alent to light. It is then clear how better our world will be when knowledge dominates our society; especially in Nigeria and Africa at large. There is need to jump into the role of shining light on every area of ignorance in the society. We need to make knowledge the bedrock of our nations. We should stop teaching some mundane things in our religious gatherings, be it in the churches, mosque etc. Let's shine the light in every sector of our society.

Please stay with me, as I do a more detailed analysis on this topic in the next chapter. Let's take the ride together.

NUGGETS:
FROM CHAPTER 2

1. The beauty and strength of a mountain.
2. Ignorance has become a mountain in our society.
3. Ignorance is equivalent to darkness.
4. All the ills of our society can be traced back to ignorance.
5. If the problem of ignorance is solved, almost all the societal problems will be solved.
6. Ignorance leads to destruction.
7. Ignorance is the number one stumbling block in our society.
8. It is your duty and mine to destroy ignorance.
9. If the church fails in her responsibility, what will be the hope of the society?
10. The mountain of ignorance must be pulled down.

CHAPTER 3

....

VARIETIES OF IGNORANCE

"I know one thing: that I know nothing."
(Socrates)

There is nothing wrong with being ignorant. Ignorance is not foolishness. Most people see the word 'ignorant' as abusive. They get very defensive and offended
when you tell them they are ignorant. Others use the
word in a very derogative manner, when referring to
someone as being ignorant. As a matter of fact, everyone
is ignorant. No one on planet earth knows everything
there is to know. Ignorance simply means, not knowing
something. So there is nothing wrong with being ignorant but everything is wrong with STAYING IGNO-
RANT!

The very first thing you have to do in order not to
stay ignorant, live in ignorance or live in self-deception which is also a form of ignorance, is to know that
you don't know everything. The true knowledge of the
fact that there is more to know which you do not know;
knowing that your whole life time is not enough to know
all there is to know. That awareness will keep you in
constant pursuit of knowledge and save you from living
a life of ignorance. A true understanding of this fact is
the beginning of wisdom.

Knowledge is progressive and as such must be a life
time pursuit. The more you know, the more you discover
there is more to know. The more you know the more you

know you know nothing. We do not even fully know ourselves. We do not have the full knowledge of our capacity or what we are capable of. If we do not fully know ourselves, what then gives us the illusion that we already know all there is to know? Why the self-satisfaction, smugness and complacency?

If a man like Socrates, whose work and thoughts are taught to be the progenitor of subsequent Western philosophy, to the point those philosophers before him were referred to as pre-Socratic. If he will be so conscious of his own ignorance, to the point that he said the only thing I know is that I know nothing. Then he was indeed a man of uncommon knowledge. His results and legacy speaks for itself. After so many years of his departure from planet earth, he still lives. You and I still read about this man whose fame came from the fact that he was a lover of knowledge. Hence he was exposed to the wisdom that the people in his days could not comprehend or fathom.

The first step to overcoming ignorance and living a life of constant pursuit of knowledge is living in the consciousness of the fact that you are ignorant. Knowing that you do not know it all, and there is more to know, and your whole life time is not enough to get to know all there is to know. This will set you free from self-deception and complacency. It will rather liberate your spirit, and open your mind to grab every opportunity you have to learn from other people and pursue knowledge.

Have you ever wondered why it is so difficult for so many people to admit to the fact that they do not know something? Are you one of such people who will rather argue and pick up a fight instead of admitting to being ignorant of something? If you have ever wondered about this, then you are not alone.

As a pastor for over 20years now, pastoring the largest church in Europe with over 25,000 members, I have traveled to various countries of the world organizing trainings for different kinds of people, preaching, teaching and counseling etc. I have often wondered why those three words are so difficult for people to say "I don't know", especially in Africa. People will rather say things they are not sure of with so much confidence, trying to even convince you to believe them. Why not just say "I don't know", and give yourself the opportunity to learn.

There was a case of a certain professor who was lecturing in the university. In one of his classes, one his students asked him a very constructive question which he knew nothing of. Instead of admitting to the student that he did not know, give me some time, and I will check it up and get back to you. No! This professor rather decided to pick on the student. He got angry because according to him the student is trying to prove that he knows better than he does, which was absolutely not the case at hand. He embarrassed the student and tried to intimidate him. But at the end of the day, he embarrassed himself. His ignorance was evident in the way he handled the issue, which made it obvious that he was rather intimidated by the question from the student.

If only we will just admit to the fact that we do not know it all, and ask questions in our area of ignorance, it will be amazing how many people are ready to help, teach and direct us. It is an inborn nature of man to help one another.

"All you've got to do is own up to your igno-rance honestly, and you'll find people who are eager to fill your head with information."
(Walt Disney)

I was driving to a function with my driver, when he seemed to have lost his way. He was busy struggling with his GPS, only to discover it was faulty. I asked him to stop the car; I came out of the car and asked the direction to the address that we were going to. We got so much help that day than we needed. We were actually taking a longer route with the direction of the GPS. We were directed through a shorter route and I was able to get to the function on time for my speaking engagement. If I had not decided to come down from the car to ask for direction, I wonder if I would have made it to the meeting, and if I had made it, I would have been late for my speaking engagement.

The same thing is applicable in every area of life. There will always be someone that knows better than you do in different spheres of life. No one is an Island, no one knows it all, and we all need one another. That is why we are humans, just admit that you do not know and ask. If only you will ask, you will get all the answers you need and save yourself from unnecessary difficulties. When you admit to not knowing something, you automatically open up the desire in others to teach you. You show your hunger to learn by admitting you don't know and then asking to be taught. A wise man is always willing to learn and will always ask questions

The only reason why people find it difficult to admit to the fact that they are ignorant is ignorance; ignorance in the form of pride, arrogance, superiority complex, foolishness etc. I am yet to hear of any great man who was not studious and very open to knowledge. Ignorance is a great limitation while knowledge is power! Choose what you want. Some say knowledge is difficult and expensive but I bet you, the price you pay for ignorance is far higher than the price you pay to get knowledge. The price for ignorance is a life time of pain and regret. Do not allow yourself to be trapped in that web. GET KNOWLEDGE!

DIFFERENT KINDS OF IGNORANCE

There are twelve types of ignorance I like us to look at:

1. Human ignorance
2. Natural ignorance
3. Ostentatious ignorance
4. Hypnotic ignorance
5. Willful ignorance
6. Cultural/traditional ignorance
7. Learned or higher ignorance
8. Sincere ignorance
9. Accepted ignorance
10. Ignorance of ignorance
11. Fearful ignorance
12. Moral ignorance

HUMAN IGNORANCE

This particular kind of ignorance is legitimate. This kind of ignorance does not occur as a result of not seeking knowledge or information, but rather as a result of the absence of the information. It is information you do not know even after you search or do your researches. A perfect example of this is when the disciples asked Jesus of when the end will be. He responded to them saying, it is not for you to know.

And He said to them, It is not for you to know times or seasons which the Father has put in His own authority.

Acts 1:7

What Jesus meant here was that the information has been kept away from man by God. It is not for you to know, I cannot give you this information. In another instance Jesus said no one knows, even I do not know except the father.

But of that day and hour no one knows, not even the angels in heaven, nor the Son, but only the Father.

Mark 13:32

So there are a lot of things that we might never get to know as humans, no matter how hard we try. For instance no one knows the very time and place he or she will die. No one knows for sure what the future holds for him/her 10 years from today. No pregnant woman knows the very moment she conceives, "I mean the time the sperm penetrates the egg and fertilization occurs". No one knows what a child that is born today will become in 40 years' time, where he will be or who he will marry. No one knows the destiny of another person, only God knows.

So in these instances, man is ignorant. Man is limited; this knowledge is not made available to him/her. The creator wanted it to be so in order to make some areas of our life unpredictable. In that way, we can learn to trust and be dependent on Him. Therefore nothing is wrong with being humanly ignorant. Human ignorance is being ignorant of information that cannot be known; more like a knowledge that is sealed and kept away from humanity.

NATURAL IGNORANCE

Natural ignorance is the ignorance of natural occurrences. Most times the true causes of flood, earthquakes and other natural disasters are not known. Just like we are yet to find permanent treatment to some human diseases today like HIV, AIDS, etc. But due to fact that researches, studies upon studies are being made as regarding it, they can be found in the future. Some years back, malaria was a very deadly disease because the treatment was not known. Thanks to medical science today malaria is one of the diseases that can be treated easily.

Natural ignorance is somewhat similar to human ignorance but totally different. While there is no possible information or knowledge available in the case of human ignorance, information and knowledge is available in the case of natural ignorance; just that is not yet known, as such it has to be discovered. Knowledge on its own is progressive. The more you pursue it, the more discoveries you make, the more information you get, and the more knowledge you have.

OSTENTATIOUS IGNORANCE

Have you ever come across people who are ignorant of a topic, but will pretend to know so much about it just to impress you? If you have, then welcome on board because you have had an encounter with someone suffering from ostentatious ignorance. These set of people, always fall into the trap of lying, just to cover up for their ignorance; which eventually exposes them in an embarrassing manner.

One of my assistants once told me of a lady she met, with a friend of hers. They were discussing the different countries they had been to. This lady by name Sarah who literally have not traveled out of her country before, and also has little or no knowledge about current affairs, countries and their different cities felt the compulsion to add to the conversation just to impress them that she had also traveled.

She told her friend that her last trip was to the Bahamas, and the friend was like wow! I am yet to visit the Bahamas. How is the Bahamas she asked? Sarah went on describing all kinds of things and how she enjoyed her stay in the Bahamas. Then she asked Sarah, what city in Bahamas did you visit and she says Texas. Texas? She exclaimed! To which Sarah affirmed yes Texas. There is no city called Texas in the Bahamas, 'Texas is in the USA' my assistant said to her. Of which she argued claiming that was the name of the city she visited. She was very embarrassed as they ended their conversation and went their separate ways.

This is the kind of situation most of our teenagers and youth find themselves in today. They are always in the need to impress and "feel among". As such they will never like to admit their ignorance, they will rather keep quiet than ask questions on a subject they know nothing about, just because they want to feel important before their friends.

Another side to this Ostentatious ignorance is that which is driven by peer pressure. Peer pressure often aligns with remaining in ignorance. Becoming knowledgeable or competent gets framed as "selling out or kissing up" Then it pays to act clueless both for show and to avoid being ostracized. Appearing stupid gains validation from the marginalized subculture of disenfranchised citizens. We must avoid the people-pleasing syndrome, be open to asking questions about what you do not know, that is the only way you gain knowledge. Parents should help their kids and teenagers by encouraging them to ask questions. Let them know it is better to be humble and learn than to be proud and live in ignorance.

HYPNOTIC IGNORANCE

This type of ignorance always results from a negative perception of self. Schooling, grading, parenting and classmates can give us the impression that we cannot learn. We discover we are damaged. Our memory, concentration or ability to comprehend new information does not work like it should. We don't digest, internalize or assimilate what we try to learn. We have fallen under an evil spell or become captivated by an oppressive narrative. We believe what we have been told about being defective, deviant or deficient. We have internalized abuse in a way that disables our natural curiosity, creativity and connecting proclivities. How we've been framed creates a barrier to new concepts.

As such the parents, school system and teachers should be careful of the kind of remarks they make on different students. Students should rather be encouraged to do better; some students who might need an extra push should be given such, instead of tagging them as mentally retarded. The future of so many children has been destroyed by these stupid and ignorant assertions from parents, teachers and schools or from people they hold in high esteem. That a student is not good in a course does not make that student a retarded person in anyway.

A perfect example of such case was that of late Dr. Myles Munroe of blessed memory. The indigent condition of Munroe's family obviously affected his early academic life. He was in school on a certain day when a teacher, apparently flustered either by his performance or conduct, told him he was nothing and would never amount to anything in life.

Young Munroe was shattered and disconsolate by the hurtful remark. He ran home weeping and then, falling before his mother, repeated what the teacher had said to him. His vibrant and faith-filled mother immediately quelled the storm of despair raging in him. She held him very close, shook him and said, "First of all, don't you ever say that again." Thereafter, she brought out her big Bible, opened Ephesians 3:20 and instructed him to go into the room and read. As Myles read the Scripture, he made the amazing discovery that God's plan for his life totally contradicted what the teacher had said. And that instantly transformed his mood and countenance. The tears disappeared, his face brightened up and he began to laugh with overflowing confidence.

Thank God for mothers like Dr. Munroe's Mum. If not for her, may be the great impact and destiny of the legend we all celebrated throughout his life time and even after his death would have been lost and wasted due to a careless statement and assertion from a teacher. Parents and teachers should be very careful and watchful of the words they say to their children.

WILLFUL IGNORANCE

Willful ignorance is "a paradoxical condition in which we are aware there is something we do not know, but choose not to know it. It is assuming ignorance when there is no ignorance." Think of it as someone putting their fingers in their ears and yelling, "La, la, la, I can't hear you." But it is also exemplified by Galileo's opponents who refused to look into the telescope, or when they did, proclaimed they saw nothing.

There is a famous reference in the Galileo affair to various people refusing to look through Galileo's telescope at the sunspots and other phenomena he wished to show them. The best known is Cesare Cremonini in the Opere, II, 564, which is a letter from Paolo Gualdo to Galileo. Cremonini had discussed Galileo's work with Gualdo and said that he wouldn't be considering it in his new book (the Disputatio de coelo). Cremonini's words were thus:

> *"I do not wish to approve of claims about which I do not have any knowledge, and about things which I have not seen... and then to observe through those glasses*

*gives me a headache. Enough! I do not
want to hear anything more about this"*
(Cremonini)

This statement by Cremonini says it all. According to him, he does not have any knowledge of it, yet he does not want to hear anything about it. How will you know if you won't listen to hear? I have not seen, yet he refused to look through the telescope claiming that it gives him headache.

Interesting isn't it? This is how a lot of people respond and react to knowledge and information today, especially when the information or knowledge is not in line with our own ideologies and dogmas. With willful ignorance people are unaware of a topic because they choose not to be informed. Willful ignorance, however, is much more insidious. There is actually something (propaganda) blocking knowledge from forming.

People suffering from this kind of ignorance hold on to their view, created by their dogmatic belief of some sorts. They are not interested in facts, this kind of people are driven by sentiments and bias emotions. They are very opinionated and are ready to go to any extent to defend their ignorant and baseless beliefs. In other not to be convinced otherwise, they will rather close their minds to the clear facts glaring at them.

The last Nigerian presidential elections gave me a great insight into this level of ignorance that is always backed up by propagandas rather than facts. I wondered in amazement, dumbfounded at the level of ignorance that my Nigerian brethren exuded. It was sure ridiculous and at the same time scary. They never bothered about facts in their arguments about the candidates of their choice for the presidential office.

Despite the facts that the previous Government failed and were totally incompetent in their administrations, so many Nigerians wanted him back. Why? On the basis that he was a Christian, he is from my tribe, and he is from my political party etc. These people never cared to look at the records of the two major candidates or to even analyze their past administrations, to know which of the candidates was more qualified.

When I presented the facts to the majority of my followers on social media, they closed their eyes to the facts that are so glaring. They choose to continue in their sentiments and propaganda. In order to make a point-less point, they resulted in abuses, quarrels and fights with one another. This is a clear demonstration of willful Ignorance. Indeed ignorance is a destructive force. THE MOUNTAIN OF IGNORANCE must be leveled in our various societies for us to be able to live in peace and have a happy world.

CULTURAL/ TRADITIONAL IGNORANCE

This kind of ignorance is propagated by a particular culture or tradition of a people based on falsehood. A false belief perpetuated by their fore fathers or a long-time way of doing things.

Just like in the case of the killing of twins in Africa before the British colonial masters came and Mary Slessor put an end to the killing of twins. It was believed before then that twin babies were witches and as such should be killed or sent to the evil forest to clean the land and prevent the family from an impending doom. They were religiously and faithfully killing these twin babies, day in day out with all sincerity without being biased. Not because they were wicked but because they were ignorant. They believed in the falsehood passed down to them, in order for them not to attract the wrath of the gods. They were seriously keeping to the terms of the gods with a clear conscience. They were not touched by the cries of these babies or their mothers.

Can you imagine the number of young destinies that were denied existence because of ignorance? So many great minds that were terminated in their infancy because of the same factor of ignorance. Ignorance indeed is a great limiting factor and as such must be destroyed if we want to live in a happier world. THE MOUNTAIN OF IGNORANCE has to be pulled down in our society.

LEARNED OR HIGHER IGNORANCE

This is the kind of ignorance that is conscious of the fact that there is ignorance on a particular area and as such is doing everything possible to get the possible solution to the ignorance. Just like in the cases of scientists, that is involved in different researches in order to proffer a solution to an unknown situation.

Thanks to this kind of ignorance and the pursuit of knowledge, we are living a better and easier life today: the invention of airplane, cars, computers, electricity etc. There are also medical researchers that embark on hours, days weeks, months and years of research to look for possible treatment of diseases without cure or permanent treatment. Thanks to them, today many diseases that medicine was ignorant of its treatment now have permanent cures.

SINCERE IGNORANCE

Sincere ignorance is an innocent and unpretentious form of ignorance, just as the name connotes. Everyone possesses this kind of ignorance in one area of life or the other. Although it is sincere, you really do not know, not because you don't want to know but because the information is not available to you yet, or you have not considered studying in that line. Even though this form of ignorance may seem to be innocent and look harmless, its consequences are grave, and individuals living in this ignorance still pay dearly for their ignorance.

> *"Nothing in the world is more dangerous than sincere ignorance and conscientious stupidity."*
> *(Martin Luther King Jr.)*

In order words, no form of ignorance is safe for you. Ignorance is not an excuse or an escape route. If you violate the law of a country because you sincerely did not know it was against the law that will not stop you from being punished by the law.

Most teenagers like to use the word "I didn't know" as an excuse for not living up to their responsibilities. The moment their mum asks why the kitchen is unkempt? "I didn't know" "you wanted me to clean it?" "You didn't tell me." "I didn't know this; I didn't know that..." they must be taught that in the real word, "I didn't know" is never an accepted excuse for not living up to your responsibilities. It is your responsibility to look for knowledge, you should seek to know what you don't know, study hard, go for trainings, seminars, ask questions, get a mentor etc. You are the one responsible for your ignorance, no else is. Therefore you have to take responsibility for yourself.

Can you imagine working with a staff that will expect you to tell him or her everything before they do it? That will be the most frustrating person to work with. People who cannot use their mind, who cannot think for themselves talk less of others. There is no creativity to them; they only do what they are told and nothing more. They will never go out of their way to do more than was required of them, and if you dare ask why, they jump to their favorite excuse, "I did not know you wanted me to do that." We must learn to take responsibility for our ignorance, thereby seeking relevant knowledge in all our endeavors. Let's not be comfortable in ignorance!

ACCEPTED IGNORANCE (REJECTED KNOWLEDGE)

In as much as all forms of ignorance are bad, dangerous and have consequences, permit me to say that accepted Ignorance is the worst form of ignorance. This is a type of ignorance that is not open to change or new ideas. They will rather stick to their way of doing things even though they can clearly see that it is wrong and detrimental to them and the society at large. The most popular phrases of the people suffering from this type of ignorance are "that is the way we usually do it, it is our culture, it's our tradition, it's our way of life and doing things, you can't change it, that is the norm". They are so comfortable with what they are used to doing that they reject knowledge no matter how good the idea you are bringing to the table.

They are self-sufficient and the most difficult set of human beings to work with. They usually feel they know it all and that their idea is better; they are caught up in a world of their own, often times very myopic and pessimistic. In the real sense of life, they know little or nothing. THE MOUNTAIN OF IGNORANCE is a force of destruction!

> *"There is a principle which is a bar against all information, which is proof against all arguments and which cannot fail to keep a person in everlasting ignorance. That principle is contempt prior to investigation."*
> *(Herbert Spencer)*

IGNORANCE OF IGNORANCE

Ignorance of ignorance is a sincere pathetic case of ignorance in my opinion. It is one thing to be ignorant and you know you are ignorant. It is another thing all together to be ignorant and not know you are. In this case, the person will be operating in all confidence without any form of awareness of their ignorance.

The only person that can look for solution to a problem or ask for help is someone that is aware that there is a problem. When you are not in the knowledge of your problem, you do not stand a chance to get a solution. In this case, the problem at hand is ignorance. Since they are not aware of the fact that they are ignorant, there won't be any need to seek knowledge. They won't even value it when given to them on a platter of gold.

The people living in this kind of ignorance always live an average life. Often times they are in a world of their own, where their ideas are best. They can easily see something wrong with what someone else did, but will never see their own wrong. Anyone that thinks differently from them must be wrong. If you do not agree with them on an issue then you are just been proud or idealistic. The only way another person can be right is if the person agrees with their ideas. This is always because of their limited knowledge. Ignorance indeed is a MOUNTAIN that has to be leveled in our society.

"Not ignorance, but ignorance of ignorance, is the death of knowledge"
(Alfred North Whitehead)

FEARFUL IGNORANCE

In this type of ignorance people will avoid knowledge, just because of the fear of the unknown that might come with the knowledge. I have heard of people that refuse to check there HIV status because of fear. According to them they will rather not know their status, than to check and discover that they are HIV positive. There are so many more circumstances that some will rather remain in the dark than know about.

These people suffering from this particular kind of ignorance love the false comfort that this ignorance gives to them. And as such, they will trade the pursuit of knowledge to have that comfort. In the real sense though, this false comfort is actually nothing but self-deception in the highest order, because they end up in more pain and disappointment at the end of the day.

MORAL IGNORANCE

This kind of ignorance occurs when people attribute the reason for occurrences to God, and will not bother to look for the reason why it happened or the possible solution to it. They will rather sit back and pray to God for help. They believe that whatsoever is happening is inevitable, they will therefore not look for solutions.

In time past in Africa, when a flood occurred, they attributed it to the fact that the gods were angry. Therefore they would do a human sacrifice to appease the gods. If someone drowned in a river, then the gods had taken the person. If there were no good harvest of crops from their farms then the gods were not happy with the land etc. All kinds of things you cannot even begin to imagine.

Today however, most people still seem to be living this kind of lie, especially Christians. Just that in their own case they do not attribute it to gods but to God Almighty. They can pray from morning to night, fasting for months but they will not work or seek for knowledge. Yet they are expecting God to make them billionaires right from their prayer room with no effort whatsoever. Their hard work is sitting down to pray from morning to night, Monday to Monday, months in months out.

Don't get me wrong, I am not in any way against prayer. I am not saying prayer is not good; I am a man of prayer myself. But if prayer is the only thing you do without working, I think you are living in ignorance, even worse self-deception which is also a form of ignorance anyways. Faith without works is dead!

Thus also faith by itself, if it does not have works, is dead. But someone will say, "You have faith, and I have works." Show me your faith without your works, and I will show you my faith by my works.

James 2:17-18

Sometimes, I imagine how disappointed God is at this kind of ideologies. It is so sad that most believers do not know what their responsibilities are, in this very age they are still expecting God to send down manna from above. That is not going to happen anymore, the season of manner is past it is now time to plant and harvest. Get knowledge, which is the only solution and true antidote to ignorance.

THE GREATEST IGNORANCE

The greatest ignorance is when God's laws are ignored. That is when ignorance has reached its worst point. That is when innocent ignorance transforms into sin. Ignorance by itself is not a sin, but ignorance of God and His laws often results in sin.

All of mankind have sinned in ignorance. We've all done something that we didn't realize was a sin until later. Maybe it was breaking our promise to God or loving others. It may have been coveting or telling lies. Whatever it was, we broke God's law in our ignorance and therefore sinned, since sin is breaking God's law (1 John 3:4).

Now some may argue that they are in the clear because they didn't know any better. However, a crime is a crime, whether the person knew better or not. God Himself said that a sin in ignorance is still a sin, making provisions for if "a person sins unintentionally against any of the commandments of the Lord…" (Leviticus 4:2).

In Acts 3, the apostle Peter was preaching to a crowd in Jerusalem about the sacrifice of Jesus Christ and repentance. He just finished telling them about Christ's sacrifice and said, "Yet now, brethren, I know that you did it in ignorance, as did also your rulers" (verse 17). We all are responsible for crucifying Christ because we all have sinned (Romans 3:23). Peter told them to "repent therefore and be converted, that your sins may be blotted out, so that times of refreshing may come from the presence of the Lord" (Acts 3:19). They still had to repent of the sin, even though they did it in ignorance.

RESISTANCE TO KNOWLEDGE

Poor attitude to self-education, Laziness to do research, no zeal or desire to learn, closed mindedness to new information, rejecting an idea or taking sides with an idea you have no detailed information and understanding of, making blanket statements without proofs and propagating propaganda has become typically the benchmark of the day.

People are so vulnerable today to falsehood because they would not do any research for themselves. They will rather depend on what someone else says. The masses have become rumor bearers and tale tellers, propagating propaganda here and there without any basis. That someone said it does not make it right. The fact that it is in the news and announced in major television stations does not make it true.

It is time we break free from every media manipulations by seeking knowledge, doing our own research, confirming information before we believe it, irrespective of who is saying what. You have the right to your own opinion. Until you confirm it to be true by thorough search and research you are not obligated to believe anyone, especially when it has to do with sensitive issues. Stop allowing yourself to be an object of manipulation by the media.

Only the ignorant spread rumors. The average and low-class citizens of the society are the tale bearers. Always remember this, anytime you have the compulsion of saying things you are not sure of, or have a perfect understanding of, that only mediocre personalities spread rumors. The wise and successful people double check all information before they believe it, especially when it has to do with sensitive issues, concerning the nation or important personalities. Don't let yourself be a puppet in the hands of media personalities.

In the last Nigerian presidential elections, I was so appalled by the ignorance of people. How the masses allowed themselves to be manipulated by media and the men of God, bringing up propagandas that had no basis or foundation. The level of ignorance in my country of origin is heart breaking and very disappointing. It is even difficult to tell the difference between the educated and illiterates, as most educated people literally acted as though they have not received any formal education. They cannot do any research for themselves; their facts were only coming from what is in the news or what someone else said, without any proper verification to know if is true or false. Only fools live in a world of assumption without clarification, don't be one of them. Don't be an average person without substance. Let all your words be backed with facts and proofs not sentiments.

Be your own person! Double check all information. Do not worship any man, for all men are fallible. I am not in any way against honor, do not misunderstand me. Honor all men, especially those in place of authority over you. Make sure you prove all information to be accurate irrespective of whom it comes from before you act on it. Always dig deep to find out the truth behind every matter before uttering a word about it, not to talk of taking sides. You do not take sides blindly, that is a clear act of ignorance. Only failures act this way. So seek knowledge and understanding in all your endeavors, for only by these can you have wisdom and true success.

- Let the mediocre carry the rumor not you.
- Let the failures propagate the propaganda not you.
- Let the ordinary people take sides without facts not you.
- Let the incompetent live in assumptions not you.
- Let the non-achievers be manipulated by the media but not you.

My dear reader, you are supposed to be a person of integrity, you are supposed to be a pacesetter, you are supposed to be different from the masses, and you are supposed to be a leader not a blind follower. You are meant to be a light that shines in darkness. There is no way you can fulfill that purpose without knowledge, for knowledge is light and ignorance is darkness. Let us therefore pursue light in order to live a more fulfilling life! If need be, we have to start an NGO, create the awareness in schools, social clubs, churches, mosque etc. especially in Nigeria and Africa. We need to set our nation and continent free from this bondage of ignorance for every type of ignorance we have just discussed in this chapter is evident and in full existence in our nation and Africa at large.

Ignorance has a lot of dangers that comes along with it. I believe you like to see some of these dangers. In the next chapter I will be talking about the dangers of ignorance. Stay with me; let's embark on this ride together. Enjoy!

NUGGETS
FROM CHAPTER 3

1. There is no excuse for ignorance.
2. Ignorance has a high price tag.
3. That you are sincerely ignorant will not stop you from paying the unpleasant price of ignorance.
4. The greatest form of ignorance is ignorance of God and His laws.
5. Pride closes the mind to new ideas thereby resulting to ignorance.
6. It is better to own up to ignorance and ask to be taught than to pretend to know when you don't know because of ignorance.
7. Ignorance leaves you in self-deception.
8. Ignorance keeps you unprepared.
9. Let the failures propagate the propaganda not you.
10. Change is opposed by ignorance.

CHAPTER 4

THE DANGER OF IGNORANCE

"An ignorant person is, by the very fact of his or her ignorance, a very dangerous person."
(Hendrik W. Van Loon)

It is no news today the serious danger ignorance is to our society, families and individuals. Ignorance is a great bondage that deprives humanity of having a happy and fulfilled life. We have to understand this very fact; we cannot afford to live in ignorance.

Most times we tend to be comfortable, when we think we are knowledgeable. And we become careless about the ignorance of the masses. We seem to forget that the masses make up our country. There can be no country without the people. And there can be no growth and civilization in a nation without the growth and civilization of the individuals (the people).

When we have a bunch of ignorant people living in a nation, it always results in having an ignorant nation. And the consequences are fatal. That is why it's not just enough for you alone to gain knowledge, we all have to make it our responsibility to educate the people around us, to educate the masses in order for us to have a nation that is knowledgeable, which will in turn result to national growth and development. Ignorance is too expensive for us to care less about it.

There aren't too many things in life as damaging as ignorance. While we've all heard the saying that "ignorance is bliss," we all know that this particular saying is about as true as "the customer is always right" - they're just words that we hear a lot. The truth is that ignorance is a very damaging aspect of our lives, and I know in many lives, it's caused a lot of pain, frustration, confusion, and aggravation. The worst times are when people act out of ignorance rather than taking the time to find out more information about a situation, and these occurrences happen much more than most people like to admit.

Another saying that we often hear is that "ignorance of the law is no excuse," and yes that's true. You will be held accountable to the law, whether you knew the law or not. What that means in essence is that it is the duty of every citizen and everyone living in a country to get knowledge of the law governing the country they live in.

Ignorance is the main force behind almost all prejudices and biases. Even the word "prejudice" implies "pre-judging," or judging beforehand, and we have to ask "before what?" The answer, of course, is before having all the knowledge necessary to judge accurately. And if you don't have that knowledge, you're ignorant, yet you're still judging. How can that ever be helpful or even be honest?

Many people who face difficult financial situations do so because of ignorance. Ignorance of basic financial principles behind credit, ignorance of tax laws and procedures, and ignorance of concepts such as interest and investing. They find themselves struggling because they just didn't know that putting so much on credit would lead to such high monthly bills. They didn't realize that even paying the minimum monthly payment on credit doesn't lower the bill enough even to make a dent in the balance. They've believed the hype behind the "buy now" mentality, and they haven't made the effort to look behind that hype and find out the true story.

> *"Ignorance may be bliss, but it certainly is not freedom, except in the minds of those who prefer darkness to light and chains to liberty. The more true information we can acquire, the better for our enfranchisement."*
> (Robert Hugh Benson)

Many religions and cults and splinter groups from major religions like to encourage ignorance among their followers, for they fear that if their followers learn more about their tenets and beliefs, they'll not like what they see and back out. In this way, these groups build intolerance and prejudice among their followers, keeping these people trapped in a system of belief that's based upon not knowing any more than the leaders want them to know. Do not allow yourself to be a victim of such groups, always seek details. Get a foundational knowledge; know all there is to know before you believe in anything whatsoever.

How many stories have you read or movies have you seen in which the main character goes through the entire film not knowing something very important, and you watch as he or she comes closer and closer to breaking through his or her ignorance to find knowledge? Aren't you just waiting the entire time for that to happen, and don't you just know that things will be much better when the character learns? In The Lion King, for example, Simba almost throws away his life and his heritage based on ignorance - he didn't know what truly happened to his father. Believing his uncle was easier than giving himself credit and finding out the truth of the situation.

How many times have you thought someone to be a jerk (or worse) because of the way that he or she talked to you or answered one of your questions, only to find out later that something bad had just happened to that person? Your ignorance caused you to judge harshly and sometimes to lose your own peace of mind, even though had you known the true situation, you probably would have reacted with compassion and caring. But getting upset is easier than thinking compassionately, until you get used to the latter.

Ignorance is the easy way out, and the easy way out is rarely the best way to take. Fighting our own ignorance takes dedication, desire, and effort. We have to learn, we have to keep open minds, and we have to step back from pre-judging based on religion, race, nationality, skin piercings, tattoos, or any other physical characteristics that lead us to depend upon stereotypes to figure out what a person is like. Ignorance keeps us down, and it keeps us from getting ahead, and the only way to combat it, is to search for the knowledge we need in any given situation. Sometimes, that's as easy to do as asking a few simple questions, but other times, it takes a great deal of effort. Either way, it's worth doing.

> *"Ignorance has a terribly high price tag — but understanding and overcoming it can really pay off."*
> (Unknown)

Never buy the first story or claim that you hear - if

you do, I can guarantee you that you're ignorant of an important side of the story that sounds much different than the one you've accepted. Don't accept first impressions, for they are based on ignorance of many other aspects of a person or place that you haven't yet seen. And please don't let prejudice ruin your life - the more we learn in life, the more open our minds are, and the more compassionate we can be to our fellow human beings who, like us, are doing the best that they can with what they have.

Also, be wary of those people who offer information or opinions about which they know little or nothing. Almost everyone is willing to offer an opinion about major news stories or political policies, even if they know almost nothing about the topic. Be quick to say "I don't know" if you know that you don't have the knowledge necessary to form a true opinion. Passing on gossip or hearsay is one of the most common, and most highly visible, forms of ignorance around.

IF IGNORANCE IS BLISS, WHY AREN'T THERE MORE HAPPY PEOPLE?

It might seem obvious... but ignorance and stupidity are life denying and dangerous. They can kill you. At the very least, they severely impact your success and happiness. Researchers have shown that those who are ignorant (uneducated) have shorter life span than their counterparts who are knowledgeable (educated).

According to the Organization for Economic Co-operation and Development (OECD):

On average across 15 OECD countries, a 30-year-old male tertiary graduate can expect to live another 51 years, while a 30 year-old man who has not completed senior secondary education can expect to live an additional 43 years. A similar comparison between women in the two educational groups reveals less of a difference than that among men.

In 27 OECD countries, on average, 80% of young tertiary graduates say they vote, while only 54% of young adults who have not completed senior secondary education do so. The difference in voting rates by level of education is much smaller among older age groups.

Education can bring significant benefits to society, not only through higher employment opportunities and income, but also via enhanced skills, improved social status and access to networks. By fully recognizing the power of education, policy makers could better address diverse societal challenges.

<u>Education brings wide-ranging benefits to the society.</u>

What is the ultimate purpose of education? Early philosophers such as Aristotle and Plato pointed out that education was central to the moral fulfillment of individuals and the well-being of the society in which they live. In the past few decades, research has supported this conventional wisdom, revealing that education not only enables individuals to perform better in the labor market, but also helps to improve their overall health, promote active citizenship and curtail violence. The analysis below presents evidence on the relationship between education and social outcomes including health, civic engagement and subjective well-being across many OECD countries.

For instance, more educated people tend to live longer...

Life expectancy reflects a long trajectory of individuals' socio-economic circumstances that affect their health conditions and other mortality risks. In OECD countries, life expectancy at birth, on average, reached 80 years in 2010. Women live almost six years longer than men, averaging 83 years vs. 77 for men.

Data shows that life expectancy is strongly associated with education. On average, among 15 OECD countries with available data, a 30-year-old tertiary-educated man can expect to live eight years longer than a 30-year-old man who has not completed senior secondary education. Among men in Central European countries there are particularly large differences in life expectancy by level of education. A 30-year-old tertiary-educated man in the Czech Republic can expect to live 17 years longer than a 30-year-old man who has not completed senior secondary education. In the 15 OECD countries analyzed, differences in life expectancy by level of education are generally much smaller among women. On average, a tertiary-educated woman can expect to live four years longer than a woman without a senior secondary education.

Ignorance therefore is not a state to be careless of; we must carry out the campaign against this deadly slow killer called ignorance. THE MOUNTAIN OF IGNO-RANCE must be brought down in our society, for us to live a healthier, happier, longer and fulfilling life. For our nation to grow, we must eliminate ignorance. For our economy to grow we must annihilate ignorance.

Ignorance is more deadly than a killer virus. You want to ask me why? Oh yes, it is more dangerous than a virus. If you are infected with a virus, you have symptoms and as such you go the hospital for medical checkup and treatment. Thereby you receive your cure, also preventing you from infecting others. But in the case of ignorance it's not so, most ignorant people are not even aware that they are ignorant. They go about distributing their ignorance to the masses freely, thereby endangering the life of many. Because they do not know they are ignorant in the first place, they cannot seek for help neither can they help those they have infected. This in turn leads to a population of ignorant people, leading to an ignorant nation and ignorant set of leaders, whose condition of living is a total reflection of their ignorance: that is poor living condition, poor economy, poor health and high mortality rate.

EFFECTS OF IGNORANCE ON YOU

These and many more are some of the effects ignorance will have on you if you permit it to stay in your life:

- Ignorance keeps you unprepared for life.
- It gives you inability to discern and plan rightly for the future.
- It limits your choices and power.
- It amplifies consequences.
- It leads to more mistakes and greater costs.

While most people would agree with this, nevertheless, the majority of people are largely ignorant of the most important things and processes in their lives. They don't know how their minds, brains, and bodies work. They don't know how they unconsciously generate their own reality, happiness or sadness. They don't know the enemies to their success and happiness. They can't even articulate their values and core beliefs, let alone improve and refine them for greater success in their life.

Such ignorance means they end up living average and unhappy lives. They make stupid mistakes that cost them peace of mind. They bounce from failure to failure in their relationships, finances, careers and health etc.

DENIAL OF REALITY

Denial of reality is one of the most common attributes of ignorance. Ignorant people do not care about facts; neither do they have respect or consider the reality. They will preferably base their beliefs on convenience. They will rather assume that everything is okay than face the facts showing that there might be trouble. One of the most life denying enemies to knowledge and happiness involves denial of reality. While philosophers might argue over it, for the rest of us, reality exists and denying or ignoring any part of it that reality can cause problems and issues in your life.

There was this group of guys driving across the desert. They drive and drive and eventually run out of fuel and became dangerously stranded in a barren and hostile environment, miles away from help. The passenger looks at the fuel gauge, which is still sitting on full, and asks the driver "Hey, how come we're out of fuel?" The driver turns to his stranded companion and says "Yeah, I don't understand it, I disconnected the wires from the gauge, and it's still showing a full tank. We should still have plenty of fuel!"

"What foolishness!" you might think. What craziness! Yet, many people live their lives exactly like that. They delete and distort their model of the world; deliberately ignoring facts and evidence until the consequences impact their lives so painfully that they can no longer deny their reality.

How many people deny the existence of God today? How many people ignore God's principles for living? How many people ignore the evidence of infidelity in their relationships? How many people ignore the warning signs of failure in some areas of their lives? The indicators of ill health or financial difficulties? Well most of us do, even though we would not like to admit it, we do on different levels and in different ways.

This reminds me of a man called Napoleon who had an excavator, a large machine used for digging dirt and soil. It was a very expensive machine and was the main component of his business. One day he was servicing it. He had the side of the machine open, when the phone rang and he had to leave it and take the call. When he returned, he saw some kids running away and noticed some sand and gravel sticking to the edge of the opening into the side-case of the machine.

Now I have to explain that this particular machine is filled with very expensive and complex hydraulic motors and pumps and sand in the internals would destroy them in a matter of seconds. Well, Napoleon decided that it would be a huge amount of work to strip down the machine and clean out any sand if the kids had thrown it into the machine. So he figured he'd just ignore the evidence and pretend that nothing had happened. He finished the service, re-assembled the machine and started it up.

In a matter of seconds, he heard terrible noises and the machine grounded to a halt. The kids had definitely filled the side-cases with sand and gravel. Now not only was

Napoleon faced with having to clean out the hydraulic system, he was also faced with the incredible expenses of replacing all the pumps, lines, filters and motors. The machine was a wreck. His denial of reality caused him even more cost and delay than if he'd faced up to the truth from the start. This was a valuable lesson for both Napoleon and for me when I heard it. Never ignore the facts. The facts are our friends!

Does this in any way sound like what is very popular in our nation today and Africa at large? We deny reality and will rather confess faith without facing the facts staring at us in the face. Forgetting that faith without works is dead. We have a way of pushing our ignorance on the devil, living in illusions and superstitions. Going to pray from Monday to Friday when we are supposed to be in the library seeking for knowledge and providing solution to the problems in our society. It is high time we wake up as a nation. The Nigerian people need to learn to seek knowledge. African continent need to embrace knowledge and begin to provide solution to her problems and stop being dependent on other continents for help.

You can never know how costly ignorance can be until you become its victim. Don't let yourself get to the point where you become its victim, because in most cases its harm cannot be reversed. The old saying "prevention is better than cure" is the attitude we should all put on in regards to ignorance and its consequences. Ignorance is such a serious disease which must be fought with all seriousness and the definiteness of purpose one can think of. THE MOUNTAIN OF IGNORANCE must be brought down.

THE WORST DANGER OF IGNORANCE

The number one danger of ignorance and the worst of it all is that we stand a chance of being rejected by God.

...because thou hast rejected knowledge, I will also reject thee, that thou shalt be no priest to me.

Hosea 4:6b

If there is any group of people God cannot stand, that group is those who are ignorant. God is no lover or companion of those who reject knowledge. He is not proud to showcase ignorant people as His servants. If you want to be used by God in a great dimension, then you must seek knowledge. God will only relate with you based on your level of knowledge. There are some people who will remain as local champions in everything they do, in all their endeavors. Well it is not a curse but what will determine your level of exposure and influence in life is totally dependent on what you know. You can never soar higher than you know how to.

If you want to be a man or woman that God will use in this season, then you must be a lover of knowledge, you must chase after knowledge as if your life depends on it, and of course for real, your life depends on it. You must obey the words of Apostle Paul to Timothy.

Study to show thyself approved unto God, a workman that needeth not to be ashamed, rightly dividing the word of truth.

2 Timothy 2:15

We must be studious and knowledgeable in all our endeavors in order not to give room to ignorance in our lives. We must have the understanding that knowledge is progressive and as such it is a life time duty. The pursuit of knowledge is what we should do until our last breathe on this planet. This is exactly the very reason for this book, to help you stay in constant pursuit of knowledge, thereby eliminating ignorance from every sphere of your life.

In the areas of existing ignorance, there are few steps I will like you to take in order to overcome it: the first step is awareness. The next step is gaining and expanding your knowledge. Finally, you have to put your acquired knowledge into action. Through practice you will achieve new skills and mastery.

The first step to breaking free from ignorance as said above is being aware of the fact that you are ignorant. When you are aware of this fact, it becomes easy for the next step to come in, which is seeking knowledge. You have to expand your knowledge scope in your area of ignorance. Finally, you should constantly practice what you have learnt from the knowledge you have acquired. With constant practice and putting into action your newly acquired knowledge, ignorance will have no choice but to give way.

Knowledge and choice provide power and control. By instilling in your unconscious mind a desire for learning, and a passionate move to repulsion of ignorance and deception, you can make an incredible life-enhancing difference to your happiness and fruitfulness in life.

Dear reader! I like to appeal to you to make a decision today to live an ignorance-free life. Don't procrastinate! You can make that decision now, and you will be embarking on your journey to a more fruitful, effective and a happy life. To help facilitate your decision making, I like to invite you on a journey with me to the next chapter, where I will be talking about ignorance as a force of destruction. LET THE JOURNEY CONTINUE!

NUGGETS
FROM CHAPTER 4

1. Ignorance is a great bondage that deprives humanity of having a happy and fulfilled life.

2. Ignorance is the easy way out, and the easy way out is rarely the best way out.

3. Fighting our own ignorance takes dedication, desire, and effort.

4. Ignorance of the law is no excuse.

5. Many people like to use their ignorance as an excuse, and the words "I didn't know" are their favorite words of all.

6. Ignorance leads to living in self-denial.

7. Ignorance keeps you unprepared for life.

8. God cannot stand the ignorant.

9. Never ignore the facts. The facts are our friends!

10. The first step to eradicating ignorance is awareness.

CHAPTER 5

....

IGNORANCE A FORCE OF DESTRUCTION

*"Of all destructive forces in this world perhaps,
known greater exist than sincere ignorance."*
(Kelvin Bache)

There is no greater self-destruction than living in ignorance. Ignorance itself is a force that destroys. Ignorance is a force that destroys? Isn't that a bit going too far and harsh to say? Some people might argue. How can ignorance be a force that destroys? Ignorance is simply not having knowledge of something and nobody knows everything after all. Well as right as that may sound it still does not change the fact that ignorance is a force that destroys. Are you surprised or do you still doubt this fact? You don't need to be; just stick with me and soon you will be convinced of this fact.

An old adage in my place says, **"What you don't know will not kill you"**.

Really...? While growing up I actually thought there was a sense in this statement used as an excuse for ignorance. But looking back now, I see how wrong that adage is, especially from the context it was used. For example, if someone drinks a glass of water that is not good enough for drinking and on seeing the person drinking, you call his attention, "oh no that water is not for drinking is dirty". The usual response from most of the adults is "what you don't know will not kill you".

I am amazed at the high level of deception I see now when I look back at those sayings. Maybe because it was not a strong poison that kills immediately, if not do you mean to tell me that if you drink a glass of acid unknowingly that the acid will not destroy your gastrointestinal system simply because you did not know? Well we all know what will happen to you immediately and there is no argument about that.

This to me is the greatest form of illusion and I wonder how many people are living in this kind of deception daily, maybe not directly in this form but in other forms. Hence they are comfortable with their ignorance and will not make efforts to get knowledge in their areas of ignorance. Nothing limits and destroys a person like ignorance, the painful part of it all, is the comfort most people take in ignorance. I have heard people say things like; "it's better I don't know about it, or I'm better off not knowing about it" Well these statements are common in our society today. The mere thought of people living this way makes my heart heavy.

Dear reader! You have to understand that:

• There is no excuse for ignorance.
• There is no hiding place in ignorance.
• There is no safe place in ignorance.
• There is no beauty in ignorance.
• There is no favor in ignorance.
• There is no prosperity in ignorance.
• There is no health in ignorance.
• There is no assurance of the future in ignorance.

- There is no success in ignorance.
- There is nothing positive about ignorance.

Do not be deceived, pursue knowledge and save your-self from the doom of ignorance. Ignorance was one of the major problems that God had with the children of Israel, their ignorance made His heart bleed. Do you know that even God cannot help you in your place of ignorance? God will only relate with you based on your level of understanding. Someone might say well He is the almighty God he can do anything he wants to do, He can help anyone he wants to help. But sorry to disap-point you my dear friends, God will not be able to help you above your level of knowledge. He won't even speak to you beyond your level of understanding because even if He does you will not understand Him anyways. God Himself aired out this frustration in the scripture below:

My people are destroyed for lack of knowl-edge. Because you have rejected knowledge, I also will reject you from being priest for me; Because you have forgotten the law of your God, I also will forget your children.

Hosea 4:6

I will like us to concentrate on the first sentence of the scripture above. "My people are destroyed for lack of knowledge". This is God talking, He called them His people, yet He could not help them because they were ignorant. My people perish for lack of knowledge. Can you imagine that! Wait a minute, these are God's people still they are perishing for lack of knowledge and God cannot help them out because they are ignorant. **What a**

force Ignorance carries! What a limitation!

Can you begin to imagine the kind of force ignorance has in your life if you let it stay? It will even prevent God from helping you. If God is now helpless in your situation, who on earth can be of help to you? You are by this force of ignorance a dangerous person to your own self. You cannot even help yourself because this destructive force of ignorance has made its abode in you.

Do you now understand why ignorance is a force of destruction? If yes, then you have to take a decision not to make ignorance your companion. You have to strive for knowledge in every area of your ignorance. You have to consciously pull yourself from the comfort zone of ignorance, knowing that there is no comfort in ignorance in the first place. You are the only one that can decide the kind of life you want to live. Do you want a life that will be destroyed by ignorance or do you want a life that will perish as a result of ignorance? The choice is yours to make. Each time I read this particular scripture it leaves me wondering the weight, the magnitude of effect and the force of destruction ignorance can have in the life of a person who embraces it.

"My people perish for lack of knowledge" of a fact these people are not perishing for lack of money. These people are not perishing for lack of food. These people are not perishing for lack of shelter. These people are not perishing for lack of clothing. These people are not perishing for lack of peace in their nation. This people are not perishing because they are under captivity. They are perishing for lack of knowledge. Wow! This is deep. If I'm to paraphrase that scripture, it will be "My people perish for their ignorance" Do you really understand the weight of this scripture? Let's take a look at the meaning of the word perish. What is perish?

Perish means: To die or be destroyed through violence, privation etc. to pass away or disappear; to suffer destruction or ruin; to suffer spiritual death.

From this definition of perish we can now see the weight or the force that ignorance possesses. Mind you this is God talking, not man. To let you know the seriousness of the topic we are talking about. Ignorance should not be taken lightly, for it is a serious force that destroys anyone that makes it their companion. Ignorance indeed is a mountain in our world today. THE MOUNTAIN OF IGNORANCE must be pulled down.

Ignorant people are helpless under the force of ignorance, even though they will not want to admit it, still it does not change the fact that they cannot live or do any better than what they know. We have to understand that: The quality of your life is not determined by your country of birth. The quality of your life is not determined by your skin color. The quality of your life is not determined by the place you live. Rather the quality of your life is determined by what you know. You can never live better than your level of knowledge. Hence the essence of good living and happiness in life is only found in knowledge.

Every problem we have in our society today is as a result of ignorance. It does not matter what you might think the cause of the problem is; the root cause of all problems in our world today is ignorance.

- Ignorance leads to pride and self-delusion.
- Ignorance leads to individual disputes.
- Ignorance leads to national disputes.

- Ignorance leads to international war.
- Ignorance leads to national disasters.
- Ignorance leads to religious wars.
- Ignorance leads to death.
- Ignorance leads to environmental pollution.
- Ignorance leads to terminal diseases.
- Ignorance leads to family disputes and divorce.
- Ignorance leads to sexual perversion.
- Ignorance leads to economic crisis, etc. to mention but a few, for the list is enormous.

> *"Because there is no greater evil than ignorance and the destruction of genius. Ignorance has been responsible for more death, more bigotry, and more sin than any other force. It is the destroyer of mankind."* (Richelle Mead)

Indeed ignorance is a force of destruction. It is a force that might not be controllable some times, because in most cases those who are ignorant do not know they are ignorant. Or better still they believe their act of ignorance is the right thing to do, or that they are fighting the right cause.

In most cases of ignorance, these people believe they are doing a great service for God. As such it becomes a force that no one can really contend with, because these people will readily give their lives up for that cause. It is no longer a question of what they like or not, it is for them a question of what they have to do to fulfill their cause. The force of ignorance pushes beyond their common sense of reasoning. When the force of ignorance is at work in an individual, common sense is displaced; this person neither reasons nor thinks clearly anymore because the force of ignorance has clouded his mind.

A perfect example is in the case of the ISLAMIC EXTREMIST, such as ISIS, Boko Haram etc. How can a human being find pleasure in killing another human being without a second thought, just because they do not believe in what he or she believes in? This destructive force of ignorance leads into an unusual desire and quest for control.

> *"The more ignorant a man is the more he thinks he ought to govern someone else."*
> *(Lewis F. Korns)*

The force of ignorance operating in these individuals gets them ready to even sacrifice their own lives in the process, just to make sure that people of a different belief from theirs are killed. The force of ignorance has persuaded them beyond any sense of reasoning. It is this force of ignorance that has given rise to: Suicide bombers, terrorism, war, Hatred, Human killing, etc.

Many motives are cited for suicide bombings, from religious sanctification to revenge for Western foreign policy to hatred of Israel, but one thing ties them together: the boast that Muslims love death, whereas their enemies love life. From killing the infidel enemy through suicide attacks, to allowing the subordinate female to participate in suicide attacks, a pattern emerges. And just as honor killings are a perversion of the most basic of human ties, so love for martyrdom takes societies into a direct relationship with the darkest side of human nature. In trying to explain this, it may be feasible to identify routes to a possible solution.

Origins:

Iranian Hossein Fahmideh was the first suicide bomber. He threw himself under an Iraqi tank with a grenade in his hand during the Iran-Iraq war. Fahmideh was made a national hero, and following his death, thousands of young Iranians carrying "keys to paradise" walked and ran across minefields, killing themselves for god and the Islamic regime.

Since the 1980s, killing oneself deliberately has become the most popular method of attacking and killing one's enemies in countries including Iraq and Afghanistan, in territories such as Chechnya or the West Bank and Gaza, and even in Western countries such as the United States and Great Britain. The first suicide attack occurred against a Western target when a bomber drove a vehicle packed with explosives into the lobby of the American embassy in Beirut. Apart from himself, he killed 63 people: 32 Lebanese, 17 Americans, and 14 visitors. Iran denied all involvement in the attack, but its protégé, Hezbollah, soon claimed responsibility, and it was subsequently established that the killings had been approved and financed by senior Iranian officials. The Iranian role in many subsequent suicide bombings has been crucial, given the existence of a clerical elite that inherited a deeply-embedded Shi'i cult of martyrdom, whose traditions of flagellation, public weeping, passion plays, martyrdom sermons, and hagiographies of martyrs were pushed into overdrive after the revolution of 1979.

An Islamic Paradox:

By 2008, 1,121 suicide bombers had carried out attacks

in Iraq, killing on a massive scale. With the exception of Sri Lanka, where the Tamil Tigers used the tactic, suicide bombing has become an almost exclusively Islamic phenomenon. Whether religiously observant or driven by other motives, the bombers have been Muslims, regardless of their country of origin. Even Islamic-raised and educated ones in non-Muslim countries (like Britain's 7/7 bombers) who are exposed to cultures without overt jihadi propaganda have put on explosive belts and gone to their deaths in order to kill nonbelievers.

This is a clear case and a perfect example of IGNORANCE A FORCE OF DESTRUCTION in operation. THE MOUNTAIN OF IGNORANCE! There is nothing anyone can say to eradicate this force of ignorance. The only force greater than this force that defeats it any day anytime is KNOWLEDGE. Knowledge is the only stronger force that pulls down the force of ignorance and we have to arise to the challenge of putting an end to ignorance in our society by distributing knowledge in every area of ignorance. Keeping in mind that, Ignorance is darkness, knowledge is light.

> *"Knowledge will forever govern ignorance; and a people who mean to be their own governors must arm themselves with the power which knowledge gives."*
> *(James Madison)*

There is always a power that comes with knowledge as we can see from the words of James Madison. This is the power we are supposed to equip ourselves and our society with, if we hope to break loose from the destructive force of ignorance; knowing that knowledge will always govern ignorance. Light (knowledge) always has a greater power over darkness (ignorance), darkness can never over shadow light. Therefore, there is hope for our community, there is hope for our society, there is hope for our nation, there is hope for our continent, and there is hope for our world!

Nevertheless, we cannot fold our hands in hope, we have to rise up and set out to war against the deadly force of destruction. THE MOUNTAIN OF IGNORANCE! This destructive force creeps into the life of its victims without them been conscious of its presence in their lives. It a destructive force that comes into the life of an individual in an innocent form, it usually appears to be innocent when it starts. You could hardly think of its ability to hurt a fly not to talk of human beings.

> *"The evil that is in the world almost always comes of ignorance, and good intentions may do as much harm as malevolence if they lack understanding."* (Albert Camus)

A clear example of the destructive force of ignorance at work will be in the case of the Boko Haram operations in my country of origin recently. Let's start by looking at what Boko Haram is.

WHAT IS BOKO HARAM?

Boko Haram is a branch of the Islamic State of Iraq and the Levant. It has been active in Nigeria since 2009. The name of the group means "Western" or "non-Islamic" education is a sin. The group is active in the northern part of Nigeria, and wants to impose Islamic law as the only law in Nigeria.

If you have been following the news about Nigeria in the last two years, you will be surprised at the different levels of destructions, killings, bomb blast that has been caused by this group. It is no news that the only force fueling this group is ignorance. It is amazing to know what effect ignorance can have on the minds of people.

How can you explain the fact that in this 21st century, a group of people will come up with the fact that western education is a sin, as such will engage in killing, kidnapping, bomb blasting to fight against western education? That is the height of insanity and ignorance in action. What else could be responsible for such act, if not ignorance? THE MOUNTAIN OF IGNORANCE! Ignorance has become a strong force of destruction in our society today.

It is like we are having a harvest of destructions in our nation today; various forms of destruction caused by ignorance surrounding us on different levels.

- Destruction in values
- Destruction in faith
- Destruction in the pulpit
- Destruction in elders
- Destruction in youths
- Destruction in people
- Destruction in government
- Destruction in our environment
- Destruction in our health sector
- Destruction in the medical sector
- Destruction in transport sector

• Destruction in our society etc.

All these destructions are as a result of ignorance. THE MOUNTAIN OF IGNORANCE! The harvest of destruction caused by ignorance has become a force to reckon with in our country, continent and the world at large. That is why it is dangerous for me and indeed for anyone to keep quiet at the site of these calamities. THE MOUNTAIN OF IGNORANCE MUST BE PULLED DOWN!!! Knowledge is the answer.

Welcome to the end of part one of this book. I hope you have been blessed so far. Stay with me as we continue our journey to part two of this book where our first topic of discussion will be "Ignorance the number one challenge of the Church". You are welcome on board!

NUGGETS
FROM CHAPTER 5

1. Ignorance is a destructive force that appears to be harmless.
2. The destructions in our society today can all be traced back to ignorance.
3. The only solution to ignorance is Knowledge.
4. The power of knowledge is greater than the force of ignorance.
5. You can never live better than your level of knowledge.
6. The force of ignorance leads to extremism.
7. Ignorance is limitation.
8. The harvest of destruction in our continent is caused by the force of ignorance.
9. Ignorance is the reason for war.
10. It is dangerous to keep quiet about the calamities in our societies caused by ignorance.

PART 2

IGNORANCE
IN THE CHURCH

CHAPTER 6

....

IGNORANCE THE NUMBER ONE CHALLENGE OF THE CHURCH

"The church must be reminded that it is not the master or the servant of the state, but rather the conscience of the state. It must be the guide and the critic of the state, and never its tool. If the church does not recapture its prophetic zeal, it will become an irrelevant social club without moral or spiritual authority." (Martin Luther King Jr.)

The biggest challenge the church is having today is ignorance. Ignorance has invaded the church hence the results we are presently having in our society today. The church today has become like a servant of the state, too afraid to question or to rise up against the ills of our society. In the words of Martin Luther King Jr. the church must be reminded of her place and duties as regards the state. The church must once again pick up her relevance by standing for her values and by enforcing these right values in our society.

Ignorance is the only force limiting the influence of the church in the society. The church a once respected institution has lost her respect due to ignorance. The darkness of ignorance has invaded the church, the very institution that was meant to be a light to her society is now covered with darkness.

What exactly happened to the church? How did ignorance creep into the church? How did the church loose her light to ignorance? Where did the church go wrong? If we can give a sincere answer to these questions, then we are on our way to getting our solution. If the church is going to regain back her position in the society today, then we have to sit back, do a total analysis and answer the above questions sincerely. In my view, the general answer to that question is the church has lost her focus. Hence Ignorance has become an exalted mountain in the Church.

What most churches especially in Africa, Nigeria to be precise sees as influence in the society is having branches of their church everywhere in the city and outside the nation, that is their idea of ministerial success and influence. How farther from the truth can that be? It is now a common fact that in most of these churches their members are not trained and equipped to discover their callings in life. Every eloquent person in church is automatically a pastor and expected to start a branch of the church in other to be celebrated. Pastors lay so much pressure on these members to the point that they give in, even though they know this is not what they want to do.

I was told that these pastors make it compulsory for any of their members going abroad to start a church, whether he wants to do it or not. They do not care to know about the purpose of these members if they are fulfilling their calling or not. They are rather more concerned about their own personal aggrandizement; listing the number of countries they now have branches as an achievement among their colleagues. If the members are unable to do this then they are seen as failures and ostracized. Because of this fear, the members do all in their power to be in the good book of their pastors even when they are struggling and living out of the will and purpose of God for their lives.

What I do not understand is where exactly these pastors got this kind of doctrine from. What scripture teaches this kind of human abuse and manipulation? Why have we lost focus of the great mandate we were given? Greed is the simple answer.

Do not for any reason allow any human being no matter what they call themselves, pastors, bishops, prophets etc. to push you into doing what you know God is not asking you to do or you don't find joy doing. Don't obey man and disobey God in the process. Your first allegiance should be to God and your purpose in life. No man is meant to dominate another man, so get up and take your life back. At the end of the day, the only person you are answerable to is God and not man.

WHAT THE CHURCH IS SUPPOSED TO BE

Now if you will ask me of my understanding of what a church is supposed to be, I will say Church as I know it and the kind of church that I am building, is the breeding ground for deliverers. So the church is supposed to be the breeding ground for deliverers. A place for training, a ground for preparation after which the individuals are released into the society, to bring the kingdom of God to the different spheres of life.

The church is not just a place we have made it to be today. We have spoiled the God's concept of the church.

We have abused His understanding of what he created. I'm afraid if Jesus comes today, He will be in trouble recognizing the institution He had established. The Church! We have over institutionalized the church. We have over organized it. We have modeled it according to our understanding. We have modeled the church as we perceived it to be, not as God perceived it to be.

From the numerous times of my being alone with the Lord, in fellowship with Him and seeking His face, I have come to discover that Jesus intended something totally different for the church, than what we have modeled the church to be today. The church of Jesus Christ was planted in this world to be a change mechanism for the transformation of the world, and of the particular society where it is located in.

- The church is not supposed to be just one of the clubs in a given society.
- The church is not supposed to be just one of the additional institutions that are required to be in a society.
- The church is supposed to be that powerhouse, the arsenal that is transforming the society!
- The church is supposed to be the center; that steering that is directing the movement of the society!
- The church is supposed to be that motor that is inspiring and igniting the life of that society!
- The church is supposed to be the center piece of any given community!

But we have lost it; we created membership and became satisfied with it. We say to ourselves, I have my members, what else do I need? I have 1000 members, I have 3000 members, I have 5000 members, I have 10000 members and we brag about it and become comfortable. **Big deal! Is it?**

But in God's mind, He is thinking, I brought that man/ woman to your church so you will help me train them and send them back to the society to do the reformation Jesus Christ started to do while he was on the earth. He started so that we might continue. He did not finish the work; He just began so that we might see the example of what we are called and created to be doing in His name. That is why we are called Christians, Christ-like, those that continue the work of Jesus Christ on the earth, and those that continue Jesus' life. We are supposed to be Christ's extensions.

The church is supposed to be the breeding ground for deliverers. In God's understanding we are supposed to be training every man and woman that steps into our church and release he or she back into the society to do things that will cause transformation in the society.

The church is supposed to be an encounter ground where people are supposed to be having encounter with the living God. The church is to be a place where the fire of God is burning, like the mountain top where Moses had an encounter with the living God and became a deliverer for his generation. The church is supposed to be that meeting place with the almighty God, where people are turned from being timid, irrelevant, insignificant individuals into people who are now filled with the holy fire of the Holy Ghost. People full of confidence, full of faith in the God who is able to do everything, in the God who has come to live in them, who has empowered them to make them deliverers like Moses was.

The church is supposed to be that place where you encounter God, and become changed by Him so much so that you become totally convinced that you are the deliverer the world and your generation is waiting for. We as believers are all deliverers sent to different spheres of life on different scales to bring deliverance to that area for God. Everyone has that internal ability and potential to cause a change, irrespective of the size.

- Maybe you might not be able to change your world, but you might be able to change your continent.
- Maybe you might not be able to change your continent, but you might be able to change your country.
- Maybe you might not be able to change your country, but you might be able to change your state.
- Maybe you might not be able to change your state, but you might be able to change your city.
- Maybe you might not be able to change your city, but you might be able to change your community.
- Maybe you might not be able to change your community, but you might be able to change your neighborhood.
- Maybe you might not be able to change your neighborhood, but you might be able to change a family.
- Maybe you might not be able to change a family but you might be able to change an individual.

It does not matter if what you have been called to do is on a large scale or small scale. Whatever your calling is, wherever you have been called to change or influence, the bottom line is that you have been called and sent by God. You have been delivered by God. You have been filled with God in your spirit. God has been revealed to you. He equipped you so that you might know Him so well, as to know that by you God will continue to improve the lives of people individually and the society at large.

CHURCH MEMBERSHIP MYTH

The Church today seems to be ignorant of its number one purpose for existence; which is the transformation of people and the society. The church has rather embraced the four walls of a building. Disassociating herself from the society, she was created for.

Church membership and the size of Church has become the driving force of most ministers today. Their pride and fulfillment seems to be in the number of people they have in their Church. They measure their success by the number of membership they have. The size of their congregation is a big deal to them. This is ignorance of the highest order. THE MOUNTAIN OF IGNORANCE! Don't get me wrong, I am not against having members, or having a large congregation. As a matter of fact, our church is the largest Church in Europe, with over 1000 branches in 50 different countries. Our church in Kiev alone has over 25000 members which are 99% Caucasian. So it is clear that I am not against large membership.

What I am talking about though, is making membership your number one goal. Making it the primary purpose of the Church, some pastors even go as far as not letting the members of their Churches go for missions because they don't want to lose their membership. They will rather keep these members in the four walls of the Church. Separating them from the society they are meant to influence. No teaching whatsoever on the role of the Church in the society. What ignorance! THE MOUNTAIN OF IGNORANCE is the number one challenge of the church today.

I do not allow anybody to just sit in my church. Everybody knows that he/she is a deliverer to somebody. The pastor should have discernment to be able to know what every member can do potentially. If you do this, your church will automatically reproduce itself. One of the major assignments of the pastor is the ability to see every single member's potentials and capabilities. Maybe the member came to the church as a drug addict. Maybe they came to the church as alcohol addict. Maybe they came to the church frustrated and dejected. Maybe they came to the church poor and rejected. Maybe they came to the church hopeless.

It is my duty and obligation as a pastor to make them believe that God sent them to this world to make a difference. That God has a major plan for their lives, irrespective of their challenges today. God can still use them for His glory. Letting them know, that God can use them to restore other people in the society to Himself. It is the duty of the pastor, to open every members mind to the sphere of the society where they have been called to take for God.

No one was just saved by chance. We are all saved to save others and to save our land. God has a specific plan for the life of every believer. It is the duty of the pastor, to open their eyes to this plan. As a pastor, you are not supposed to cage your members in the four walls of the church, all in the name of membership or church activities. What a pity! It is due to this ignorance that the Church has lost her influence in the society today. Because we have failed in raising the believers in our churches, equipping them with the word of God, the principles of the Kingdom and releasing them back into the society to change their world for Christ. This is the heart beat of God and the primary purpose of the church.

But what has most present day church done? They look for every manipulative means to keep people in church in order to get them to keep paying their tithes and offerings. I was amazed when a protégé of mine told me how her father was refused burial from a church in Nigeria he has been part of for over two decades stating that he was not paying his tithe or some dues in the church. I was perplexed to discover that churches do keep records of those who pay tithes or not, those who give large or small offerings. This to me is rather ridiculous! These are the kind of things these pastors and churches use to cage their members to the four walls of the church, so they can be in the good book of the church. Why should we reduce the purpose of the church to such an irrelevant and baseless interest? Ignorance indeed has become a mountain in our churches.

A CHURCH OR A CULT

It is amazing to know, or come to the understanding of the kind of practices we have in some of our churches today. When I hear some stories of the present happenings in the church, it makes me weep in my spirit. I can't help but ask myself, is that a church or a cult? Can you for a second imagine a church setting, whereby you have to do only what the man of God is telling you to do or saying. It does not matter if he is wrong or right. As long as the man of God said it, you have to do it.

A church filled with the traditions of men. A church filled with "bundle of dos and don'ts". A church filled with the doctrines of men that have nothing to do with the principles of God. Just because they want to be in control, they disembogue controlling spirit on the congregation, overshadowing the church with it and sabotaging the liberty of brethren. There is no liberty for the members to do what the Holy Spirit is asking them to do, without the permission of the "man of God". What exactly is going on in the Church today? The bible says in the presence of God there is liberty.

Now the Lord is the Spirit; and where the Spirit of the Lord is, there is liberty.

2 Corinthians 3:17

I cannot help but wonder what kind of spirits are in these Churches. Is it the Spirit of the living God or a spirit from the pit of hell? I was once told a story of churches that do not allow their members or junior pastors to write books, especially in my country of origin Nigeria. This is barbaric! Ignorance in operation!! THE MOUNTAIN OF IGNORANCE!!! When I asked what the reason was, I was told that there is nothing God will tell the junior pastor to write about that He cannot tell the man of God. So they are not supposed to have a different vision but to support the vision of the man of God and the ministry.

Can you begin to imagine the kind of limitation these "men of God" are placing on the wonderful resources God has placed in the Churches, just because they want self-aggrandizement?

What kind of doctrine is that? Where is that coming from? Who told you that because you are a pastor, God is obliged to reveal all information to you alone and not your members? What gives you the impression that you are better than all your members or anyone else for that matter? Is the Holy Spirit in you different from the Holy Spirit in them? This is a pure satanic strategy to limit the Church. It is quite unfortunate that the pastors that are meant to be representing Christ are buying into this ignorant deception because of pride and the pursuit of fame.

God does not use only one person, irrespective of who you are, or the title you are bearing. Whether you are a pastor, prophet, evangelist, bishop, pope, etc. let it be known to you that God has a specific plan for all His children. What you are called to do is to train and equip them to discover what they are called to do and encourage them to step out and do it. If God is giving any of your members a topic to write on please encourage and guide them. Never make yourself an obstruction to your members as regards fulfilling what God is asking them to do. Please do not kill the visions of these young ones. Don't stop them from doing what God is asking them to do. Remember you will give account to God for your every action.

SPIRITUAL AUTHORITY OR SPIRITUAL DICTATORS

I like to start this paragraph stating it clearly that I am not against Spiritual authority. I believe in it because I believe there should be order in the church. What I am against though, is pastors hiding under the umbrella of spiritual authority and becoming dictators to their members. They decide for their members where to stay, who to marry, what to do and what not to do, where to live and where not to live. Their members have to take permission from them before they can travel. Some even go to the extent of monitoring their member's tithes, how much they pay and how frequent they pay. This is ridiculous! Ignorance at its peak!! THE MOUNTAIN OF IGNORANCE!!!

The bible said those who are led by the Spirit of God are the Sons of God, not those that are led by their pastors.

For as many as are led by the Spirit of God, these are sons of God.

Romans 8:14

Leave people alone to live their lives. Your only duty as a pastor or leader is to guide and advise the people when needed. Pray for them and allow the Holy Spirit to lead them. Even the Holy Spirit does not force His will on us, He only directs, guides and leads us. Who then are you to try to force your will on people?

When the bible said we should have dominion, it was not dominion over man. We are to dominate the earth and every other creature not man. Stop manipulating people and allow them to fulfill their God given purpose in the society. Only in that way will the limitation on the church be lifted, and the church can regain her relevance in the society again.

MISPLACED CHORES FOR CALLING

It is a pity but sadly this is what is happening in the body of Christ today. I believe most of us will be familiar with this: have you ever asked someone - what is your calling or ministry? And the person responds, "I sing in the choir, I work in the sanctuary unit, I am in the welfare department, I am an usher, I play instruments etc." Or maybe you are the one that was asked and you mentioned one of the above listed as your calling or ministry.

Permit me to ask you a question, how many of you do not go to work, I mean pursuing your profession and carrier because you have done your house chores? As much as your house chores are important, will that stop you from going to work? But this is exactly what we do in the house of God. We replace our callings with the chores we do in the church. Every ministry you are oper-ating in, in the church is like your home chores, house-keeping. Which is very good but that cannot replace your calling. As much as doing the chores in the house of God is very important, that should not replace your calling. The same way doing your house chores does not stop you from going to work, the church chores should not also stop you from going into the society and fulfilling your calling.

Pastors, your members need to be taught what their callings are. It is your responsibility to help them discover it and encourage them to fulfill it. Church activities should never replace their God given purpose. Every believer has a specific area God has called them to, outside the four walls of the church. Empower them and send them out to fulfill their purpose. Let's break the yoke of ignorance in this area, in order to liberate the church from the present challenge of irrelevance the church is facing because of THE MOUNTAIN OF IGNORANCE.

Every member of our church knows their calling. They know who they are called to, where they are called to, and we encourage them to pursue it. I do not allow anybody to just sit in the church without them influencing the society for God in their area of calling. If a person came into our church as a musician I tell him/her, you are not just called to play in the church band, because that way you cannot change the world. You only impress people in the church and you think you are a hero. You have to do it in the society out there. If you are called into the world of music, know that you are not just called to minister in the church; it is a particular vocation, a particular area of life, in this case music. If that is your calling, you should know it is your gifting from God.

Then it means you have to improve it, polish it, get prepared, get educated, get secular knowledge and divine knowledge (God's knowledge), develop your skills, so that your gifting can become your platform. Through that platform you will be able to speak for God and bring the dominion of God, the influence of God into that sphere of life in that particular city or society where you are living in.

Some people have a local calling, a city wide calling,

a national calling or an international calling. Not everybody has an international calling though. But wherever you are called to you should know it. If it is in the area of music, then that is your field where you are called to, so you have to minister there.

"Not everybody can be famous but everybody can be great, because greatness is determined by service." (Martin Luther King Jr.)

In my church, everyone who is a musician has a ministry outside the church. Apart from playing in the church, he/she will have a ministry where they can have home groups for some worldly musicians.

The bible said we are the light of the world not of the church. We are the salt of the earth not of the church. Our light is supposed to shine in the world that is where darkness is. The church already has enough light. So take your light to the world, because excessive light can result in blindness. It is this blindness that leads to believers fighting among themselves concerning who holds which positions in the church. When their right positions are outside the church, where they are supposed to shine even brighter than they can ever shine in the church. Why? Because light is much more appreciated in the presence of darkness, so let's take our light to the world where it will be more appreciated and thereby bringing glory to the name of Jesus. Yes we are supposed to be the salt of the earth because it is sour out there not in the church.

Some of us are called to bring change to the music industry. But do you know what we have done? We have incorporated it into our churches. By staying in the church and singing our Christian songs and building a wall around us, we restrict ourselves to the church, thereby segregating ourselves from those we are supposed to minister to. We have become useless as light of the world and salt of the earth. Because all the people we are ministering to are already salted, when you salt something that is already salted you are over salting it.

Instead of you to bring delight and deliciousness, you bring saltiness and irritation. That is why we end up irritating one another in the church, and that is why our churches keep on splitting. We are getting mad at one another and we get dissatisfied running from one place to the other, looking for what is not lost. This is because we are supposed to be trained in the church and get our platform in the world but rather we want to have our platforms in the church. And since you cannot salt what is already salted and get a benefit from it, we just end up irritating one another.

- We have missed it brethren!
- You are the salt of the earth not church!
- You are the light of the world not church!

Come out from the four walls of the church and shine to the world. Come out of the four walls of the church and salt the world. The world needs your sweet savor and flavor. YES THE WHOLE WORLD IS WAITING FOR YOU!

You are the salt of the earth; but if the salt loses its flavor, how shall it be seasoned? It is then good for nothing but to be thrown out and trampled underfoot by men. You are the light of the world. A city that is set on

a hill cannot be hidden. Nor do they light a lamp and put it under a basket, but on a lampstand, and it gives light to all who are in the house. Let your light so shine before men, that they may see your good works and glorify your Father in heaven.

Mathew 5:13-16

Instead of us (believers) going to lighten the world, to salt the earth, to change and transform the society, we rather go to the society to get jobs and to make a living. We are not sent by the Lord Jesus Christ to go and make a living and work for salary. As much as that might look legitimate, that is not the primary reason why you should be working. Thinking that way is a whole lot of confusion. We are sent into the world for a different purpose, even when you have a job in the world, it should not be for the purpose of the salary but for the platform. Your job therefore should become the platform through which you stand to proclaim and reflect the Lord Jesus.

When you go there to work for salary and daily bread, you lose your regard. That is the reason while they don't have any respect for you, they can even tell you to keep quiet. You might have been working there and nobody knows you are a Christian, or they might know but just despise you, because you are not seeing yourself as God sees you. You do not carry yourself with the consciousness of who you represent. You make yourself equal to them as coworkers, but you are not supposed to. For you are an ambassador of Christ sent from heaven to redeem the earth. You are the hope of the world. You are alive and they are dead, but you don't act like it, you look like them, you struggle and strive for the same thing they strive for. Working to make a living should not be your purpose. It is just the benefit that comes with it.

My purpose on the earth is to reveal the savior in me, thereby saving others. I am sent to the world to be a deliverer to somebody. I am sent to the world to be a savior to somebody. I become the light of God to the world. The profession that I have is supposed to be a platform from where I could be able to be efficient, to be efficient in my calling from God to represent Him. My priority as a believer is to depopulate hell and populate heaven. That is the believer's essence for living. We live for God and not for daily bread.

- Oh no, we have lost focus of what we are called to do.
- We have lost our identity.
- We are ignorant of our placement in God.
- We have become ignorant of our responsibility as a church.
- Pastors no longer have a sense of purpose and obligation to the flocks of the Lord Jesus Christ.
- The mountain of ignorance has become a great challenge to the body of Christ today.
- This mountain (THE MOUNTAIN OF IGNO-RANCE!) has to be pulled down

WE HAVE USED THE NAME OF JESUS TO BUILD AN EMPIRE FOR OURSELVES BECAUSE OF IGNORANCE.

What an irony! Ignorance has penetrated into the church of the Lord Jesus Christ. Ignorance has cost the church her respect. The church has lost its influence in the society because of the same ignorance. The same institution that was created to emanate light has become the store house of darkness. The church that was supposed to be a place for raising kings and kingdom imposers on the earth has turned to be a place of raising slaves.

Our kingdom is a kingdom of kings and priests. But our pastors have subjected those who were called to be kings in the society as slaves in the four walls of the church. They have succeeded in raising a bunch of servants that do not know what the purpose of their master is for them. They are taught to sit in the church and serve, and thereby being useless to the society. The church's ignorance has separated her from the affairs of the society, the very society they were called to be light and salt to.

The church has lost her voice to ignorance and religion! What happened to the church of the Lord Jesus Christ? Ignorance has crippled the purpose of the church that Jesus originally had in mind. The Church has made the size of membership her ultimate goal. They are very comfortable with the size of their congregation hence, limiting the purpose of the church. Nothing else seems to matter but the number of people they have in their congregation.

The church is almost located at every corner of our society especially in Africa, Nigeria to be precise, yet evil reigns in our society. Why? It is because the church has lost her influence to ignorance. The Church has separated herself from the society. For example, Texas is ranking among the most corrupt states in the USA, mean while having the highest number of churches. Big churches with famous preachers, this is a big shame to the body of Christ.

> *"Wherever the early Christians entered a town the power structure got disturbed and immediately sought to convict them for being 'disturbers of the peace' and 'outside agitators.' But they went on with the conviction that they were a 'colony of heaven' and had to obey God rather than man. They were small in number but big in commitment. They were too God-intoxicated to be 'astronomically intimidated.' They brought an end to such ancient evils as infanticide and gladiatorial contest. Things are different now. The contemporary Church is so often a weak, ineffectual voice with an uncertain sound. It is so often the arch supporter of the status quo. Far from being disturbed by the presence of the Church, the power structure of the average community is consoled by the Church's silent and often vocal sanction of things as they are."* (Martin Luther King Jr.)

The church is not supposed to be a place we come to just to feel good. The church is not supposed to be a place where we just come for healing. The church is not supposed to be a place we come to when we have one need or the other. As much as all those are good, that is not the primary purpose of the church. The only reason you should feel good and be healed is so that you can go back into the society and reflect Christ. But rather the church has become a breeding ground to a bunch of needy people who only come to church because of their needs.

We have succeeded in raising people that are a bunch of users. Users of God who do not care about His needs. They are only in church seeking the hands of God and not His face or ways. All we have in our pews today are a group of needy people, all due to ignorance. They do not know any better and as such cannot do any better. That is why the church remains in the quagmire of her needs, because she has made what is supposed to be last as the first and has made the first become last. Ignorance has led to misplacement of priorities.

No one can serve two masters; for either he will hate the one and love the other, or else he will be loyal to the one and despise the other. You cannot serve God and mammon. Therefore I say to you, do not worry about your life, what you will eat or what you will drink; nor about your body, what you will put on. Is not life more than food and the body more than clothing? Look at the birds of the air, for they neither sow nor reap nor gather into barns; yet your heavenly Father feeds them. Are you not of more value than they? Which of you by worrying can add one cubit to his stature? So why do you worry about clothing? Consider the lilies of the field, how they grow: they neither toil nor spin; and yet I say to you that even Solomon in all his glory was not arrayed like one of these. Now if God so clothes the grass of the field, which today is, and tomorrow is thrown into the oven, will He not much more clothe you, O you of

little faith? Therefore do not worry, saying, 'What shall we eat?' or 'What shall we drink?' or 'What shall we wear?' For after all these things the Gentiles seek. For your heavenly Father knows that you need all these things. But seek first the kingdom of God and His righteousness, and all these things shall be added to you.

Matthew 6:24-33

Every believer, every member of our church is a potential deliverer in the society. But if you don't open their eyes to it, they will never know. This is the duty of the pastors and leaders of the church, to open the eyes of the people to their calling in God and their placement in the society. They have to be taught, they have to know, that consciousness has to be built into every individual.

When we just get satisfied with taking tithes and offerings from them, comfortable with the size of our church then we miss the whole idea of Jesus Christ. I can imagine Jesus weeping in Heaven, because we are making the people He placed in our care useless for the Kingdom. We have raised a bunch of Christians, saved, having the power of God inside them, having the Holy Ghost in them, yet they are useless to the society. The society is deteriorating daily because we have spoiled the purpose of the church through Ignorance. We have succeeded in aborting the purpose of the Church through our ignorance, yet we are complaining against abortion.

We must break the shackles of Ignorance from the neck of the church; we must bring back knowledge into the church today. The devastating stories I hear from our churches today is rather shameful. Yes it is rather outrageous that Pastors will fight among themselves over members. And members fight among themselves over who occupies what position in Church. My God! What exactly is going on? IGNORANCE HAS BECOME THE NUMBER ONE CHALLENGE OF THE CHURCH TODAY.

The church is ignorant of her purpose. Pastors are ignorant of their purpose. Members are ignorant of their purpose. Pastoring has become a means to survive for many pastors today. They have become seekers of their stomach instead of seekers of God. The Church has become like an organization, where membership is a big deal. The number one concern of pastors today is the number of people they are able to gather as members. Ignorance indeed is a challenge to the body of Christ today.

IGNORANCE LIMITING THE CHURCH

I once heard a story of a particular minister, who had a word from God to start a movement in the community, and he went to share his vision with his pastor, instead of this member getting an encouragement from his pastor, he was rather discouraged by him. The pastor asked him not to, that it is not of God. "If it was of God, God would have told me. Besides the ministry cannot have two visions, the only primary vision is the one God has given me". According to the pastor, all this young minister has to do is to sit in church and support his vision.

These are the kind of pathetic stories surrounding

our churches today. For some of the members that are even courageous enough to step out in faith to obey God, they are ostracized by the church and the pastor. Some even go as far as laying a curse on these members. What a shame! Whoever told you, you have a monopoly to having a vision? What part of the scripture ever told you that God cannot speak to the member without passing through the pastor? Whoever gave you the ministry of cursing other brethren? This is a big blow of ignorance in the church of today. We have lost the purpose of the church. The church is supposed to be the breeding ground for deliverers, and not slaves.

> **But on Mount Zion will be deliverance; it will be holy, and Jacob will possess his inheritance. Deliverers will go up on Mount Zion to govern the mountains of Esau. And the kingdom will be the Lord's.**
>
> *Obadiah 17, 21*

On mount Zion shall be deliverance. Where is mount Zion? Mount Zion is the church. From the Church there will be deliverance to our families, neighborhood, community, society, city, nation, continent and our world at large. Deliverers will go out of mount Zion to govern the mountains of Esau. That is deliverers will go out of the church to govern the different spheres of the society and only then the kingdom will be the Lord's. Let's not allow ignorance to make the church work against the purpose of God for the church. For it is our duty as a church to uphold the dignity of its purpose through knowledge.

ONLY KNOWLEDGE CAN BREAK THE CHAL-
LENGE OF IGNORANCE OFF THE NECK OF THE
CHURCH.

> *"The church must be reminded that it is not the master or the servant of the state, but rather the conscience of the state. It must be the guide and the critic of the state, and never its tool. If the church does not recapture its prophetic zeal, it will become an irrelevant social club without moral or spiritual authority. If the church does not participate actively in the struggle for peace and for economic and racial justice, it will forfeit the loyalty of millions and cause men everywhere to say that it has atrophied its will. But if the church will free itself from the shackles of a deadening status quo, and, recovering its great historic mission, will speak and act fearlessly and insistently in terms of justice and peace, it will enkindle the imagination of mankind and fire the souls of men, imbuing them with a glowing and ardent love for truth, justice, and peace. Men far and near will know the church as a great fellowship of love that provides light and bread for lonely travelers at midnight."*
> *(Martin Luther King Jr.)*

As Christians and as a church, we all have to take a leaf from Martin Luther King Jr. Let's be bold to represent God in our different spheres of life where God has called us to, even if it means giving our lives for the purpose of God to be fulfilled. God is looking for more

Martin Luther's of our time. Will you be the one? Let's all make ourselves useful for the kingdom.

> **For whoever desires to save his life will lose it, but whoever loses his life for My sake will save it.**
>
> *Luke 9:24*

It is high time we place God's purpose for our existence above life itself. We have to break off from the shackles of fear and ignorance, embracing knowledge and courage. Only then can we take the nations for Christ.

Let the Church arise!

NUGGETS
FROM CHAPTER 6

1. The Church is the breeding ground for deliverers.

2. Our kingdom is a kingdom of kings and priests, not a kingdom of slaves.

3. Are you a spirituality authority or spiritual dictator?

4. We have succeeded in raising a bunch of needy Christians.

5. We should stop using the name of Christ to build empires for ourselves.

6. You are the light of the world not the Church.

7. You are the salt of the earth not of the church.

8. The Church is your training ground, the world is your platform

9. We are called to influence the society not to remain in the four walls of the church.

10. Ignorance is the number one challenge and a limiting force in the Church today.

CHAPTER 7

....

WHEN THE CHURCH IS IGNORANT OF HER PURPOSE

"I can't stand your religious meetings. I'm fed up with your conferences and conventions. I want nothing to do with your religion projects, your pretentious slogans and goals. I'm sick of your fund-raising schemes, your public relations and image making. I've had all I can take of your noisy ego-music. When was the last time you sang to me? Do you know what I want? I want justice – oceans of it. I want fairness–rivers of it. That's what I want. That's all I want."
(Martin Luther King Jr.)

I believe you are conversant with this popular saying, "when the purpose of a thing is not known abuse is inevitable". Could that be the situation with the church today? Is the church truly ignorant of her purpose? Is the church truly being abused? Unfortunately the bitter truth about it is yes. The church has been abused. Yes, the church seems to have lost knowledge of her purpose. So it is a capital YES!!!

The church is ignorant of her purpose and hence the purpose of the church has been abused. As a result of this, the dignity and the respect of the church have been lost to ignorance. The church no longer has a say in the society anymore, because the church has lost track of her purpose. The church is now chasing shadows. The church that was supposed to be a place of mighty warriors, is now a place filled up with timid bunch of voiceless people.

> *"Things are different now. The contemporary Church is so often a weak, ineffectual voice with an uncertain sound. It is so often the arch supporter of the status quo. Far from being disturbed by the presence of the Church, the power structure of the average community is consoled by the Church's silent and often vocal sanction of things as they are."*
> *(Martin Luther King Jr.)*

No other factor could be ascribed to this effect except for the fact that the church of today is ignorant of her purpose. The church is ignorant of the course for which it was created. In the early church wherever the Christians got to, they were known because of the influence they brought upon any society they walked into. They were called **"the people that turns the world upside down."** Why was it so? Because the world is full of darkness and wherever the believers got to, they brought light with them, which in turn upset the darkness that overshadowed that city and turned it down. That was the way it was. The voice of the church was heard. The church was not indifferent to the happenings in the society. The early church was not timid; they were bold in declaring the standards of the kingdom and in shedding light in every area of darkness.

And when they could not find them, they dragged Jason and some of the brothers before the city authorities, shouting, these men who have turned the world upside down have come here also.

Acts 17:6

The early churches were known to confront the ills of the society. They were the conscience of every city they were in, a voice that calls the nation to order. They never kept quite at the torts going on in the society. Even to the point of death, they challenged the violation of the principles of God. They never kept to the societal status quo. They had only one standard and that standard was the Bible. What then have become of the church of today? How did the church get to this point? The only perfect answer to this question is the fact that the church of today is IGNORANT OF HER PURPOSE.

This is the whole reason for the rise in immorality in our societies today. The moral degradation in our nation is totally due to the very fact that the church is ignorant of her purpose. The church has been secluded from the world, the very place they were meant to be a light to. What a pity!

In the month of July 2015, I came across a famous preacher that was interviewed concerning the situation of the Supreme Court ruling that legalization of gay marriage in the 50 states of America. To my amazement, I heard a phrase from this famous preacher that left my heart broken. He said "THE WORLD WILL ALWAYS BE THE WORLD AND THE CHURCH WILL ALWAYS BE THE CHURCH". I was totally disappointed by this statement. Where exactly did we bring this doctrine from? This doctrine of separating the church from the world, if the church is to be separated from the world, then why is the church in the world? Jesus said I am the light of the world. He did not say I am the light of the church. He said He was the light of the world.

> **When Jesus spoke again to the people, he said, "I am the light of the world. Whoever follows me will never walk in darkness, but will have the light of life.**
>
> *John 8:12*

That is the same ministry that we all are called into. We are the light of the world. Light is meant to shine in darkness. The darkness is in the world and that is where we are supposed to be shining our light. Jesus was never indifferent to the darkness in the society in His time and He definitely does not expect us to be indifferent to the darkness in our society today. The church is the institution that is supposed to shed light into every area of darkness in our society. We are meant to be the voice that we rise against every evil that is perpetrating its ugly head in our society. We are supposed to pull down the stronghold of darkness through the light that is in us. We are not supposed to stand on the fence as the church has now resulted to doing; simply because we want to be politically correct. We want to be accepted by the society.

Jesus rightly said that, until the gospel of the kingdom is preached to the whole world, the end will not come. Which simply means this is the very ministry Jesus left with us believers. Not only that we are the light of the world, but we are supposed to take the light which is the gospel of the kingdom into the whole world and not just in the four walls of the church.

And this gospel of the kingdom will be preached in the whole world as a testimony to all nations, and then the end will come.

Mathew 24:14

It is therefore our duty to bring the light of the gospel of the kingdom into the whole world, thereby eradicating darkness. Whoever told the church that her ministry is in the four walls of the church? What then is the church without the world if "the world will be the world and the church will be the church?" in the words of the American famous preacher. Why then are we in the world? Why then did Jesus die for the world?

For God so loved the world that he gave his one and only Son, that whoever believes in him shall not perish but have eternal life.

John 3:16

We cannot in anyway separate the world from the church. The sheer thought of that separation shows for a fact that the church is ignorant of her purpose. We are here to bring the Gospel of the Lord Jesus Christ to every sphere of life. To reclaim the nations and the world back to God. For the earth it's the Lord's and the fullness thereof. It is therefore the duty of the church to restore back the earth to God.

The earth is the Lord's, and the fullness thereof; the world, and they that dwell therein.

Psalm 24:1

It is high time for the Church to arise to the knowledge of her purpose and take her rightful place in the society. The church today has become so insignificant and irrelevant in the society so much so that the church is taken for granted. Why? The church has lived in ignorance of her purpose. She has lost her goal for existence. The church in this present decade has resulted to chasing shadows. Things that were meant to be irrelevant are the things that are now important to the church. But her very purpose she has pushed aside, all because of this enemy called ignorance. THE MOUNTAIN OF IGNORANCE!

The major achievements of the church today are no longer the ones resulting in national transformation. Rather their greatest achievements they take glory in are: the size of the church, the size of membership, the properties of the church, the eloquence of sermons, loyalty of members, the size of crowd I pull for my annual programs, how many times I have filled the stadium for my programs. Believers have reduced the purpose of God for the church to mundane things.

Pastors have used the name of Jesus to build a kingdom (church) for themselves where they hold all the members that are supposed to be kings in their different spheres of influence as slaves, serving them in the name of membership. They have made the gospel of no effect. It has become a gospel of their stomach, satisfaction and ego. No wonder the society no longer has any regard, respect or reference for the church.

- The purpose of the church is not the erection of gigantic buildings.
- The purpose of the church is not in the size of the congregation.
- The purpose of the church is not in the size of her membership.
- The purpose of the church is not in the four walls of a building.
- The purpose of the church is not Sunday services.
- The purpose of the church is not in hosting programs, entertaining ourselves.

As much as all these things are not necessarily bad, they are not the primary purpose of the church, and as such should not be our primary and only focus.

Churches are not ready to stand up for or to anything in the society that will not profit the church or the pastor directly. It is even bad how these pastors turn deaf ears to the plight of people who are not their members. Even though they may not really care for their members at least they attend to them for the gain they will get in return.

I was told of a pastor who refused to pray for someone who was desperately in need and was being oppressed by demons. This pastor told the lady that if you want me to pray for you then you must be a member of my church. The lady told him she was already committed in another church and the pastor refused to pray for her. To which he later said, "Baboon dey work monkey dey chop" meaning I only work what I get paid for, that she should go back to the church where she is committed and let the pastor pray for her. Is this not insanity at its peak?

WHAT THEN IS THE PURPOSE OF THE CHURCH?

The church is meant to be a training ground where believers are trained, empowered and released into the different spheres of society, to bring light into every sphere of the society thereby causing national revolution and transformation. The church is to equip believers and release them into the society to restore the earth back to Christ.

This was the understanding the early church had in the days of the apostles. That is why they were pace setters and refused to settle for the status quo of their time. Where ever they were, every city they entered, people could not help but know that they had arrived. Because they had understanding of whom they were. They were not ignorant of their purpose. They knew they were the light and the whole earth was in darkness. They knew it was their duty to eradicate darkness.

Hence they were not afraid of fulfilling purpose. The government of the day could not stop them. Death threats could not stop them. Persecutions could not stop them. Imprisonment could not stop them. Difficulties they encountered could not stop them. Rejections and ostracizations could not stop them. Traditions could not stop them. Religion could not stop them. The society could not stop them. They were totally sold out to their purpose, because they had an understanding of their responsibility to their society. They worked in the knowledge and consciousness of their purpose for their society.

It is therefore the purpose of the church to be a light in our society. The church is the salt of the earth. The church is the light of the world. If then the world lies in darkness, it simply means that the church has failed in her responsibility. "You are the salt of the earth; but if the salt loses its flavor, how shall it be seasoned? It is then good for nothing but to be thrown out and trampled underfoot by men".

> You are the salt of the earth; but if the salt loses its flavor, how shall it be seasoned? It is then good for nothing but to be thrown out and trampled underfoot by men. You are the light of the world. A city that is set on a hill cannot be hidden. Nor do they light a lamp and put it under a basket, but on a lampstand, and it gives light to all who are in the house. Let your light so shine before men, that they may see your good works and glorify your Father in heaven.
>
> *Mathew 5:13-16*

It is high time the church traces back her steps to understanding her purpose. It is only through the knowledge and understanding of the purpose of the church, that the church can fulfill her purpose. That is the only thing that can make the church relevant in our society again. Yes when the church begins to fulfill her purpose, her relevance will be restored. It is therefore the duty of the believers to be the salt and light to every sector of their society. It is not just enough to complain about the problems we have in our society. It is our responsibility to fix them.

Every believer should be taught to take responsibility in every sphere of life where there is darkness. It is irresponsible for a believer to just sit down and complain about the ills in the society, when it is our duty to fix them. The first consciousness I want every believer to have is to hold ourselves responsible for the darkness in the society. That will quicken us to be more solution minded rather than sitting back to complain. Always pushing the blame back to the government and politicians is not the solution. The only people that have the solution to the world's problem are believers. The church is the anchor the society holds for restoration. The church is Gods provision for the restoration of the earth. We cannot afford to fail God. It is high time we wake up to our responsibility and shake off the shackles of ignorance from off our neck.

> *"The God whom we worship is not a weak and incompetent God. He is able to beat back gigantic waves of opposition and to bring low prodigious mountains of evil. The ringing testimony of the Christian faith is that God is able."*
> *(Martin Luther King, Jr.)*

We have to strategically look into every sector of the society, and train believers to take responsibility for the sectors that are their areas of interest; for example: Politics, Government, Economics, Education, Entertainment, Science and culture, Health, Sports, Business, Agriculture, Family, Marriage, Arts, Media, etc. In all the listed sectors above, believers should choose their areas of interest. Get trained and go back to the society to enforce the kingdom in that sphere of life.

In any area of the society we see something going wrong, the church is to take full responsibility for it by bringing light into that area of the society. We should not just sit down and complain and blame the government for the ills of the society. We should not be indifferent or complacent to the ills of the society. We have to rise up to our responsibility. The number one purpose of the church is to be a light, salt, deliverer, restorer, and builder of the man, the society and the earth.

We have to device means to correct the ills of the society. We need to have different kinds of training and teachings that will align the society back to the purpose of God for that nation. The values of the kingdom must be brought back to the society through the church. The church has to restore back her relevance by getting involved in the affairs of the society. The church cannot be separated from the world, society, and government. We have to be in the system to be able to influence the system.

How can pastors be teaching their members not to be involved in politics, that it is not of God? Yet they complain of bad governance; if the believers should not participate in national politics who then will bring light into that sector of the nation? This explains the reason why our nations and society are covered in darkness. The believers that were meant to be light have decided to hide their light under the basket, "the basket of Church".

THE EARLY CHURCH

"We need to recapture the gospel glow of the early Christians who were noncon-formists in the truest sense of the word... Their powerful gospel put an end to such barbaric evils as infanticide and bloody gladiatorial contests. Finally, they captured the Roman Empire for Jesus Christ."
(Martin Luther King Jr.)

Let's take a journey down the memory lane to see what the early church, protestant church stood for. How they were able to make a difference in their time. Max Weber was a German sociologist, economist and politician. In the year 1904/1905 Max Weber wrote a series of essays about the evolving of capitalism in Northern and Central Europe. These series of essays were later to become the widely read book called "The Protestant Ethic and the Spirit of Capitalism." According to Mr. Weber the Industrial Revolution that gave birth to the new economy in Europe and eventually to our modern civilization, was as result of the teachings of the European Protestants.

Weber believed that when the Protestant ethic influenced large numbers of people to engage in work in the secular world, in enterprises, in trade, in savings, in investments, these gave birth to the new world economy, that is largely known as capitalism. It is upon that economy that our modern world stands.

"All growth depends upon activity. There is no development physically or intellectually without effort, and effort means work."
(Calvin Coolidge)

Social scientists don't doubt the fact that the European civilization which is the civilization the whole world enjoys today, was as a result of the direct teachings of the Protestants. If the teachings of the early Christians changed Rome and the entire Roman Empire, we can't point to any great change that the teachings coming from our pulpits today are producing upon our world in general. If the teachings of the Protestants in Europe gave birth to the Protestant ethics and the modern civilization, it becomes alarming that most of our charismatic teachings today mainly concentrate on individual aggrandizement.

The kind of gospel that our churches are preaching sometimes is not powerful enough to change the very street where these churches are located talk less of the nation they live in. We are not even going to throw the challenge of changing a whole generation before the modern day church. These generations of believers don't seem to even know what that means.

The basic teachings of the Protestants were all surrounding values, ethics and morals. The Protestants teachings affected the view of the populace to work. Through their teachings they dignify even the most mundane professions. According to them any profession or work that adds to the common good of man must be respected and it is dignified. They taught the Protestants that every work is sacred as long as the believer does it to the Lord.

In their churches the Protestants taught believers to go out of the four walls of the church to demonstrate their love for God by how they serve fellow humans. The emphasis of the churches was not in how much work or home keeping is done in the four walls of the church itself, they rather told the Protestants to go prove their love to God at their work places through the quality of their works. It is believed that every work you do is unto the Lord and your love to God must show in the quality of your product. This led to a drive in everybody to do their best and produce the best possible qualities. As a result, these products were the best in the market. Eventually they became the best in the world, bringing revolution to the European economy.

The most revolutionary aspect of this teaching however, is the fact that the Protestants began to look for ways and means to serve God better through inventions, discoveries, researches, sciences, factories, industries, etc.; this lead to at first, up to 90% of all inventions of the world coming from the Protestant world. Up till recently 75% of all inventions from the time of the industrial revolution are credited to the countries where Protestant ethics were taught.

One major teaching of the early Protestants that we the Protestants of today must go back to is the fact that the European Protestants did not emphasize fivefold ministry the way we do today. Today our teaching on the five-fold ministry only tend to view only those called to the five-fold ministry as those called to be ministers, while the rest of the congregation is just viewed as laity who just go to secular jobs.

The way the early Protestants taught on the other hand is that everybody is a full time minister in their various places of work. They went to the extent of saying, your job, profession, occupation is your calling. So you're actually fulfilling your calling by going to work and giving your best. Hence, the Protestants go to work not just for the money. Their biggest motivation for work is service to God and man, not the interest to gain profit or make money.

> **And whatever you do, do it heartily, as to the Lord and not to men, knowing that from the Lord you will receive the reward of the inheritance; for you serve the Lord Christ.**
>
> *Colossians 3:23-24*

The Protestants believe in the higher power through the truth they derive from the word of God. They got to know the truth and that truth set them free, and they took the truth to the society which set their whole generation free. We too in the present day protestant church can do the same thing for our nations. God is the same yesterday, today and forever.

Thank God, the people we are talking about are not members of (the early church); they were not in the days of Jesus. Maybe if it were one of the disciples of Jesus, we would have said it is as a result of the physical impact of Jesus on their lives. These people were Christian like you and I. I strongly believe that, if the church of today will apply the same principles they applied, the church will get the same result today irrespective of location. Why am I going too far? This is the perfect example of what God is doing through our church in the Ukraine. Thousands of lives are being transformed from day to day.

The members of our church are actively involved in every sphere of the society, bringing the kingdom influence into those areas of the society. Every member of our church knows the area they have been called to, and hence have been empowered through training and teaching to go take over the spheres of the society that they are called to. It is solely due to the influence of our church that gays do not have a say in our society today. That is what the church all over the world is supposed to be like. The church was never meant to be timid. The church was never meant to be just one other institution in the society that can just be ignored.

The church is the conscience of the society and as such cannot be silent in the presence of adversities. The church cannot fold her hands and watch while evil penetrates or is continually perpetrated in the land. The church cannot be sidelined from the affairs of the society. The church cannot be separated from the world. The church cannot overlook the different kinds of pervasions that have taken over our society today.

It is high time the church arose to her purpose. The church needs to fix the different problems and difficulties in the society, for it is only in the fulfillment of the purpose of the church, that the church can find her relevance. The church was meant to be a voice of God to the nations. The church was supposed to be the very place where the nation turns to for direction. The church was meant to be the agent of change. The church was supposed to be a place of leadership for the society. The church was supposed to be a solution center to all the problems of the society. But due to the mountain of ignorance ravaging the church, the church lost the sense of her purpose. Ignorance of the purpose of the church has led to what we have turned the church to:

- We have rather turned the church to a place for self-aggrandizement.
- We come to church because of what we want to get from God.
- We come to church to have our needs met.
- Even when we give, it is like a business for us. We give to receive double or triple of what we gave to God.
- We have turned church to a place of self-satisfaction and pleasure.
- Church for us is now a place we get our desires met.
- We come to church because we want to make heaven.
- We have turned the church to an organization that is all about me, myself and I.
- We come to church for good music.
- The church has become a place of entertainment.
- We come to church to showcase what we think we have and who we are.
- Our testimonies are all about office promotion, material achievement, etc.
- We have made the church beggarly; our teachings are all centered on what we can get from God.
- We are careless of what God is expecting from

us in regards to our society.

- As long as everything is OK with my family, the society is not my business.

- The church is more concerned about fund raising, launching for church building but have no concern about the poor and the needy of the society. The problem of the society is not our problem; we have to erect a bigger building for our church.

I can imagine the heaviness in the heart of God. Looking down at us and seeing how ignorance is diverting the body of Christ from his purpose for the church. If I may ask, who ever gave you the ministry of building the church? That is not what Jesus asked us to do. "He said I will build my church".

And I also say to you that you are Peter, and on this rock I will build My church, and the gates of Hades shall not prevail against it.

Matthew 16:18

Jesus never asked us to build the church. But that is what we have turned our whole concentration to. I am not saying it is wrong to build the church. What I am trying to point out is that, that is not our primary purpose. The primary purpose of the church is to preach the gospel of the kingdom to the whole earth, to disciple the nations for Christ.

And Jesus came and spoke to them, saying, "All authority has been given to Me in heaven and on earth. Go therefore and make disci-

ples of all the nations, baptizing them in the name of the Father and of the Son and of the Holy Spirit, teaching them to observe all things that I have commanded you; and lo, I am with you always, even to the end of the age." Amen.

Mathew 28:18-20

And this gospel of the kingdom will be preached in all the world as a witness to all the nations, and then the end will come.

Mathew 24:14

This is the very ministry Jesus left for the church, the very purpose for the existence of the church on the earth. Hence the church must gain knowledge of her purpose and retrace back her steps to fulfilling her purpose. Until then the earth cannot be restored and the society cannot be saved for the church is the hope of the nations...

LET THE CHURCH ARISE TO HER RESPONSI-BILITY!

NUGGETS FROM CHAPTER 7

1. The church is the conscience of the society and as such cannot be silent in the presence of adversities.

2. Every believer should be taught to take responsibility in every sphere of life where there is darkness.

3. It is the duty of the Church to fix the different problems in the Society.

4. The purpose of the church is not the erection of gigantic buildings.

5. The purpose of the church is not in the size of the congregation.

6. The church is meant to be a training ground where believers are trained, empowered and released into the different spheres of society for positive impact.

7. The ministry of believers is not in the four walls of the church.

8. It is the duty of the church to bring back the values of the Kingdom into the society.

9. Let's take a lead from the early protestant Church.

10. The church is the voice of God to the nations.

CHAPTER 8

WHEN THE CHURCH SPREADS IGNORANCE

"Ignorance deprives people of freedom because they do not know what alternatives there are. It is impossible to choose to do what one has never "heard of." (Ralph B. Perry)

There was this story of a pretty young woman who was in labor and was taken to the hospital for the child delivery. During delivery, she lost a lot of blood and the Doctor made an arrangement for a quick blood transfusion to save her life. To the doctor's amazement she bluntly refused that she was not going to have a blood transfusion. When the doctor asked her why? She said her church does not believe in blood transfusion. All effort to make her understand proved abortive and she was still bleeding.

The doctor tried all he could in explaining to her that her life was in danger, but she ignored the doctor stating that, according to her church that blood transfusion is a sin. In frustration the doctor called in her family to explain her critical state to them and why she needs immediate blood transfusion to save her life. But they gave him the same cooled response; it is against the doctrine of our church.

The doctor, having tried all he could as regards convincing the family without any positive result; frustrated at the deteriorating sight of his patient, he excused himself and went to his office. Ten minutes later the nurse came calling the doctor, we are losing her; I can't feel her pulse anymore. By the time the doctor hurried to her bed side she was dead. The doctor covered her up and went to his office heartbroken and in tears. In the words of the doctor "I just can't stop wondering in amazement at the level of ignorance that was running in the life of this family, all in the name of church doctrine".

It would have been better if the story ended this way but no, the family took it a bit further by saying it was the will of God that she died that way. Some were crying and asking God why? Why do you have to take her away from us now? Why God? Why now? I couldn't help but ask myself, how on earth could this family comfortably shift their ignorance to mean God's will? They bluntly refused to heed the advice of the doctor in order to save the life of their daughter, and now it was God's will? Amazing! But this is a true life story and things like this happen daily in different forms. What Ignorance! THE MOUNTAIN OF IGNORANCE must be pulled down in our society for us to have a breath of fresh air.

> **My people are destroyed for lack of knowledge. Because you have rejected knowledge, I also will reject you from being priest for Me; because you have forgotten the law of your God, I also will forget your children.**
>
> *Hosea 4:6*

Nothing is so destructive like ignorance in action. Nothing limits us like ignorance. The death of this young prospective lady was due to total ignorance. Ignorance of the scriptures, ignorance of the personality of God, ignorance of His ways. The most ignorant action they took to wrap it up was playing the blame game. Putting the blame back to God, isn't that amazing to you? I kept wondering how they could turn the blame on God, asking God why? When God had made a provision available for her safety but they refused to make use of God's provision. Does that look like what we do in our various lives most times? When we refuse to take responsibility for our ignorance, but we are rather more comforted to blame God or others for our failures, disappointment and pains in life.

Well I think we all have the answer to that question, give yourself the sincere answer that will be the very first step you will need to take for your deliverance. The provision for a qualified doctor was made available. The provision of her blood type was made available for blood transfusion in other to save her. But she and her family refused the use of the provision God has made available, because of religion (church doctrine). Some of us might be reading this story now, and in our minds, we might be saying, oh what a barbaric act! But in reality that is what most of us do in our day to day life. Just that your own case is different from this one, does not exempt you from this life of ignorance that has come upon us as a result of wrong teaching from our various churches.

These kinds of story are not scarce in Africa, especially in Nigeria. Some would tell you I don't take drugs, I don't go to the hospital, I have faith, my pastor has blessed water for me to drink, all sorts of things that will beat your imagination. The same thing applies to those who will not work hard, yet are praying and believing

God to be millionaires. They have faith according to them and believe God for a miracle.

> What does it profit, my brethren, if someone says he has faith but does not have works? Can faith save him? If a brother or sister is naked and destitute of daily food, and one of you says to them, "Depart in peace, be warmed and filled," but you do not give them the things which are needed for the body, what does it profit? Thus also faith by itself, if it does not have works, is dead. But someone will say, "You have faith, and I have works." Show me your faith without your works, and I will show you my faith by my works. You believe that there is one God. You do well. Even the demons believe—and tremble! But do you want to know, O foolish man, that faith without works is dead?
>
> *James 2:14-20*

Christians in Africa and most third world countries today will rather go for prayers and fasting than go to work. Going to wait on God to do for us what he has asked us to do for ourselves. The dignity of hard work is no longer emphasized in church today. Churches teach members to seek for favor and miracle rather than putting in hard work and dignity of labor to earn their living and become successful in life.

> *"All life demands struggle. Those who have everything given to them become lazy, selfish, and insensitive to the real values of*

life. The very striving and hard work that we so constantly try to avoid is the major building block in the person we are today".

(Pope Paul VI)

HOW IS THE CHURCH SPREADING IGNORANCE?

The church has succeeded in spreading ignorance through her wrong teachings and preaching. I believe every society is a product of the teachings and preaching that come out of its pulpit, either from the church, mosque and different religious temples etc.

A perfect case study will be the African continent, especially Nigeria. Nigeria is a very religious nation; about 50 percent of the populations of the people in Nigeria are Christians. So it is clear that the church has a great part to play in the state of the nation today. In fact the church in Nigeria is part of the problem the country is having today. Oh yeah, I believe that the church in Nigeria is one of the greatest problems we have. Most people make a lot of noise about the fact that the problem with Nigeria is with leadership. That could be partially true, but when people talk about that, they usually refer to political leadership especially of the highest order. In my opinion, the leadership and the structure of the church in Nigeria are as guilty of the situation in the country as much as the politicians.

We Christians like to judge, condemn and point fingers at the politicians. In some cases some churches are worse and some of the practices in churches might even be worse than what the politicians do. Why do I think that the church in Nigeria contributes largely to our troubles? I am a strong believer in the fact that whatever is happening in any country, the number one cause of it is the damaged value system of that nation. I think we have a faulty and perverse value system in Nigeria. That is the root cause of all our problems not just political leadership. The political leadership comes from our society. Our leaders are not being imported from other countries or from some mysterious places. Neither are they coming from nations that are totally different from ours. No!

These political leaders are emerging from our culture. They emerge from our value system. They are a result of our societal virtues. That is what we produce. It is not a matter of one leader that is bad or two leaders or 10 leaders or even 100 leaders that are bad. We have been talking about bad leadership for all the 56 years of our independence; meaning our society has not been capable of producing worthy leaders.

Despite the fact that our leaders come and go in their thousands, they all still repeat the same failures, because that is what they know. That is the value they have been brought up in. That is the value they have imbibed in their system. Most of the people, who are condemning these leaders, will still do the same thing if they get to those places of authority. Since they come from the same value system they can only produce those kinds of results. Results produced out of ignorant teachings and value system that has been spreading over the years. THE MOUNTAIN OF IGNORANCE!!!

> *"One of the grate tragedies of life is that men*
> *seldom bridge the gulf between practice and*

profession, between doing and saying. A persistent schizophrenia leaves so many of us tragically divided against ourselves. On the one hand, we proudly profess certain sublime and noble principles, but on the other hand, we sadly practice the very antithesis of these principles. How often are our lives characterized by a high blood pressure of creeds and an anemia of deeds! We talk eloquently about our commitment to the principles of Christianity, and yet our lives are saturated with the practices of paganism. We proclaim our devotion to democracy, but we sadly practice the very opposite of the democratic creed. We talk passionately about peace, and at the same time we assiduously prepare for war. We make our fervent pleas for the high road of justice, and then we tread unflinchingly the low road of injustice. This strange dichotomy, this agonizing gulf between the ought and the is, represents the tragic theme of man's earthly pilgrimage."
(*Martin Luther King Jr.*)

For us to have a corrupt value system as a nation and then be hoping to produce godly leaders is hypocrisy of the highest order. It doesn't just happen! Of course you could have exceptions when individuals have worked on themselves and have refused to compromise with the order of the day. In those cases when such individuals refuse to live by the faulty values of the land, then there could be a difference. Those are in very rare occasions.

It would take a miracle to have such leaders, what

would normally happen is that even when such leaders emerge they would be largely opposed. They would be criticized because what they are doing will not make sense to most of the citizens. Most of the people on the ground profess different value systems. The value systems the reformed leaders are bringing to our society would conflict with the ones that people are used to. The people would be condemning them. The conflict equals clashes. That means there would be controversies and disagreements. These conflicts might actually lead to those governments been toppled and those leaders been removed.

I believe everything we see in our country is a product of our defective value system. A broken value system means a broken economy, a faulty growth and a damaged political system. So what is the role of the church in all that?

The truth is that our value system comes from our pulpit. Our value system comes from our religious beliefs. Our value system comes from our religious practices. Our value systems come from our educational system. In Nigeria, the authority of the religious institutions is much higher than the authority of the educational system.

Another place where our value systems come from is from the families. In Nigeria every family belongs to a church or one religious group or the other, probably a mosque; so mostly our value systems are influenced by our faith and our religion. That is why I am saying it is the faulty and corrupt messages we have introduced to our pulpits that is responsible for producing corrupt practices in our society. It is the ignorance from our pulpit that has spread to the different spheres of our society today. Hence the results we are having in our different nations in Africa especially Nigeria.

Let me give you a few examples. A Pastor could say that somebody would be a millionaire before the end of the year. Whereas we are in November or December and there are 500 people in that auditorium. All of them will shout AMEN! Yet Pastors don't correct them saying that no, you would not become a millionaire before the end of the year even if you shout amen for the whole day.

The only person that would become a millionaire is the person that has worked hard for it. It is he who has been diligent for the whole year or years before then. The only person that would become a millionaire is the person that has at least signed a contract. When Pastors don't clarify that, everybody begins to believe that some miracle would happen. So when such a member goes to his office and he sees an unsigned check for a million dollar, and nobody is claiming responsibility for it, he claims it. He believes that it is God that has provided for him.

That is how corruption gets from the pulpit to the society. That particular member would claim that God has answered his Pastor's prayer. He would boldly come to give testimony the following Sunday while the naive and ignorant members would shout HALLELUJAHS! Meanwhile they too are expecting similar miracles and on and on goes the vicious cycle of corruption from the pulpit to the whole country. This is the spreading of ignorance and erroneous teachings or preaching, on the part of the pastor and the church. This indeed is THE MOUNTAIN OF IGNORANCE!

For example the culture of Pastors and leaders of churches celebrating and praising only the rich and the wealthy, giving them special seats as though they are the most important people in the church. They are the ones who have access to the Pastor. They are the ones who have a say. They are the ones who are respected and honored mostly because they can give more. In fact I heard that in some churches right now, your access to the pastor depends on the size of your tithe or the money you bring. What does that say? It means that for me to be important even in the house of God, I must be rich. If I must be rich, then I have to, by all means. Most of these people that we are celebrating might not even be making their riches in a pure and righteous way. Maybe they are scammers and fraudsters, yet they are the ones who are celebrated in the church. That also would promote corruption.

One of the teachings I have heard in Nigeria is a teaching of breakthrough without balancing it. They don't teach that breakthrough is a result of overcoming resistance. It is a result of battles you must have fought. It is a result of having worked hard. It is a consequence of having worked diligently. You must have pushed; you must have applied some forces of labor and a lot of forces of nature, before breakthrough comes.

Breakthrough is a word from breaking forth. Water, springs or streams break forth from under the ground. For it to break forth, it must have been forcing its way for years before it suddenly breaks through. The breakthrough that we see all of a sudden is as a result of hard work, invincible hard work. Yet we don't emphasize the hard work aspect, we don't emphasize the preparation aspect. We only emphasize the breakthrough. We think that those breakthroughs only come through prayers. That is another root of corruption. Purely the spreading of ignorance! THE MOUNTAIN OF IGNORANCE!!!

Everybody goes out of the church looking for a breakthrough. So any opportunity they see, even though they are not legal, and they didn't labor for it, they want to take advantage of it. We are promoting through our preachings and teachings from the pulpits the culture of getting something for nothing. That means, "I don't need to do much, but I can get something, I can become rich". That way we are promoting corruption in the whole country. Instead of us to promote the culture of hard work before profit, we rather promote frivolity from our pulpits. Spreading Ignorance ignorantly! Instead of teaching people to pay the price for whatever they wish to get, we are saying the opposite. We teach that you only need to have faith. You don't need to labor.

In fact some people actually believe, a fallacious concept being preached in churches that "one day of favor is better than a thousand years of labor." Even though that could be true, that is not the rule. That is just an exception. The rule of life is that you work hard for your results. You don't wait for grace or favor to give you results without working for them. We don't teach people in our churches that truth. If you don't work for riches, and even if you get the riches through your parents, relatives or spouse, you are still a thief (Prov. 28:24). You are robbing the people who gave you that wealth, because somebody worked for what you are claiming. How can you just be going to church and claiming something for yourself? That is another faulty doctrine we have that promotes corruption in the country. This is ignorance at its peak. THE MOUNTAIN OF IGNORANCE!

It is ignorant to teach that people can claim anything; how can they claim when they are not qualified for it? How can they just claim something simply because they have greed for it? We are promoting greed, we are promoting lust. As Pastors when we preach those kinds of messages people believe us. Can you imagine! We are not talking about two hundred people or a thousand people; we are talking of millions who are going to church and hearing these erroneous messages every Sunday? Instead of us to have taught them that you would not receive anything that you are not qualified for. Instead of teaching them that no! It is only merit that qualifies you for gain. No! It is only excellence that qualifies you for profit. No! You don't get something without going through the process of production. Yet we keep on giving people false hope and call it faith. This is Ignorance! THE MOUNTAIN OF IGNORANCE!! It is through these ways the Church spreads Ignorance.

There is no product without the process of production. We tell people they can get something by faith, to only believe. We tell them to just give offerings. We teach them about faith offering. We teach them about tithe and offering. Not that I don't believe in tithe and offering, but that is not the way of receiving wealth. It is the way of preventing curses from coming to your resources.

For you to really have wealth, giving tithes and offerings are not enough. Tithes and offerings open up heaven to you; God doesn't send money from heaven. You have to go to work and be involved in the process of production. It is only that way wealth and riches will come to you.

But we don't teach that much in our churches. We just tell them to come to church and believe God. We say; the man of God will pray for you, just give him seed offering or prophetic offering. We believe that once he prays for you, that is what matters and it's only Gods favor that does it. WHAT IGNORANCE! THE MOUNTAIN OF IGNORANCE! The church has so much engaged in the spreading of Ignorance.

The same God whose name we are using, had set up rules and order in nature. It is God that created work. It was God who created the process of production. It was God who created all the rules and laws of life that we all need to abide by. But we always overemphasize the dependence on faith while we underemphasize the role of hard work and diligence. The church has become ignorant of the ways of God and as such is spreading this ignorance in the society through our wrong teachings.

Another problem we have in the nation that is contributed by the church, is that we teach millions of people that they should expect miracles. Pastors teach about miracles without telling them the truth about the order of life. The way we are all supposed to live on a daily basis is not through miracles or by miracles. We are supposed to live by laws and principles that God has placed in the laws of nature, in the principles of life and order. To depend on miracles is to live in Ignorance.

Life depends on laws and rules. But we tell people about miracle! miracle! miracle! No matter what you talk to a Nigerian about, they will tell you about the fact that God will do it. We are asking God to do for us what He has asked us to do for ourselves. There is no way God can do for man, what man is supposed to do for himself.

There is no way man can do for God what God can only do.

Most of our prayers as Christians are about 80 percent a waste of time. This is because we ask God to do for us what he has asked us to do for ourselves, or we ask God to do for us what He has already done. Thanks to that ignorant teaching, our people expect miracles from morning till night. Our people are looking for miracles, so any opportunity that presents itself godly or ungodly we take as God's miracle or blessing. That is a major factor encouraging corruption in the land.

In the real sense we don't teach people that the possibility of miracle is not the order of the day. It is only two percent of our daily life that should depend on miracles from God. The order of life is the observation of God's laws and order. Obedience to the laws of God and the society brings wealth and blessings. There are a lot of faulty and ignorant teachings that have been promoted through the pulpit of the church. They have led a whole generation of people who have now grown up in those teachings thinking that is the way life works. When things don't work out the way they expect, they think something is wrong with them. Ignorance! THE MOUNTAIN OF IGNORANCE!

Today, another teaching we have that is faulty and as a result of ignorance is that we tell people to just pray, as if production comes only by prayers. But in the real sense, productivity doesn't come by prayer, productivity comes by labor. It is through work that we have productivity. As a result, in Africa and especially in Nigeria, most people will rather go to church than go to work. Most people will rather spend the whole day in church, rather than going to spend 18 hours at work. Most people will rather spend a whole week or two fasting and praying. Most people go to the mountain for months, while they have an able body. We neglect the value of labor, yet we are expecting our economy to prosper. We complain about why we live so badly, is it not obvious now? Ignorance is what is killing us!

Another faulty teaching, rooted in ignorance that the church is spreading is that we tell people only God can help our world! Only God can help Africa! Only God can help Nigeria! We tell people to just keep on praying. It is not true that we only need to pray to fix things. We have been praying as Christians, especially in Nigeria. Probably I can say Nigeria is the most praying country in the world. Why is God silent to our prayers? Why is God not responding to our prayers? It's definitely not because God is wicked or God is not compassionate or doesn't like Nigeria. It is because we are using the wrong medicine on the wrong sickness. Is like you are having cancer and somebody is giving you tablets for headache. It will just make your case worse, and it won't give you any relief.

We have not told the truth to our people, our churches have not told the truth to our country. The people in government are also religious people. Some of them believe in the same unsubstantiated nonsense that is coming from our pulpit. The churches are not ready to educate the populace. I think we must set our country free from these erroneous and ignorant teachings. We must hold the church leaders and the major denominations of this nation responsible for these wrong teachings of ignorance spreading through our nations.

Instead of our churches to help our people get free from the claws of superstitions, we are rather creating our own superstitions in the church. Most of the faith in our churches that we call Christianity today is all based on superstition. I was talking to a pastor who told me he was in the village, coming back to the city on Friday. But he was telling everybody that he will leave on Monday. I said to him you are a man of God, why are you not telling the truth? I know you are leaving on Friday, why are you telling people that you are leaving on Monday? He said ah! This is Nigeria, you don't tell people your plans, because anything could happen. They could go and wait for you on the road.

This is a famous man of God that is teaching people on the television everywhere, having so much followership. Millions of people respect him, yet he is more driven by fear than faith. Although he said he doesn't believe in Satan, but his action tells me that he believes more in the power of Satan, witches and wizards, than in the power of God that he represents and the gospel that he preaches.

All these kinds of superstitions are littered all over our land. There are many other ignorant and erroneous teachings too that I cannot begin to go into now. Those are the things that hinder development and economic growth in a nation.

This has to be addressed because until we stop spreading these ignorance-rooted teachings, the world at large, especially Nigeria will never be set free. The church is supposed to bring light, but we are putting our people into more darkness. The church is supposed to be the foundation and the pillar of truth, but we are not establishing truth. We are establishing deception and Ignorance. The church is supposed to be the light of the world, but we are not bringing light. We are rather submerging our people into darkness. The church has succeeded in spreading so much ignorance in our societies today. THE MOUNTAIN OF IGNORANCE!!! For us to see restoration, growth and development in our society, this mountain of ignorance most be pulled down. We must put an end to the spreading of ignorance.

We have to get the church to be responsible for the state of our nation. The church is creating wrong value systems, defective virtues, erroneous teachings that have now made us who we are today. Every nation is a product of the messages they hear, of the information that go to their mind, and on the values system they base their decisions. That is why there is no way the church of today can abdicate herself from being responsible for all the problems in our nations. I believe that we all need to respect our men of God, the fathers of the land. We must give honor to whom honor is due. The church needs to be honored and respected, yet we need to correct these things that are wrong. We have to put an end to the spreading of ignorance by the church.

We have not done a good job regarding our doctrine. We have done a good job bringing people to God. We have been guilty of preaching word of faith doctrine, prosperity doctrine, all of which are despised in our world today. We must bring back to our society a balanced Christian doctrine. We must restore fundamental truths of Christianity that the early Protestants stood for.

These teachings are responsible for the development that we have in the western world today. The civilization we have in our age now is thanks to the sound and knowledgeable teachings of the Protestants. Our modern civilization is as a result of the Protestant ethics. Those truths are what we must return back to our pulpits, if we want to become a developed and civilized nation. If we want to end the spreading of ignorance, then we must restore back knowledge to our pulpits. We must go back to the knowledge carried in the teachings and preaching of the early Protestants that brought about civilization. We must put an end to the spreading of ignorance from our pulpits, by embracing these early protestant principles. What then were the teachings of the early protestant church?

TEACHINGS OF THE EARLY PROTESTANT CHURCH

Just as I mentioned in the previous chapter, the Protestants believed in the higher power through the truth they derive from the word of God. They got to know the truth and that truth set them free, and they took the truth to the society and set their whole generation free. Just like today, the Protestants and their teachings had to fight with the prevalent order of the day which taught that:

- Work is only for making profit.
- Make money with minimum effort.
- The culture of the day viewed work as a burden to be avoided.
- The secular world of today teaches that you should not do more than what is enough for good living.

As we can see from these points, the sinful nature of man is the same in every generation. Man naturally moves towards entropy. We are driven towards the carnal, mundane and the mediocre. We need a higher power, force and truth to deliver us from this entropic movement to self-destruction and pull us higher to greater values. When work is viewed only as a source of economic gain, the centrality of work becomes self-indulgence, selfishness and egocentrism. There is a great advantage when work and economic gain is viewed from the perspective of moral and spiritual significance.

Another very important aspect of the protestant teachings is that money is simply a byproduct, a natural consequence, compensation, it is never the goal. The quality of goods and services are always viewed as more important than the compensation. If I do my best and produce the best products, then I shall definitely be compensated. The by-product will come when the products and services are good.

I think it would be interesting for us to know from what perspective the Protestants preached faith. They preached faith not as a means of personal gain or profit. The Protestants preached that through faith we can endure. For example I need faith to keep on working on my product, I need faith to give my best, I need faith to endure the process of production, I need faith to persevere, I need faith to pay the price of self-denial, of sacrifice, of repetition. I need faith to keep myself encouraged while I go through the hardship of labor.

The Protestants preached that faith is necessary to planning. They encourage their members and followers to see into the invisible world. They taught their adherents to plan into the future and believe that they are able to bring to pass that which they have envisioned. The Protestants taught their followers that faith is needed for hard work because every hardship on its own discourages, hence you need faith not to be discouraged. The faith you have keeps you going and makes you to pass through the valley and the mountain top.

The protestant churches today need to borrow a leaf from the actions of the early Protestants. We need to preach the gospel not just from the aspect of selfish gains and profit, but from the kingdom perspective whereby we strive to build the kingdom of God through each believer on the earth as it is in Heaven. We have to preach this knowledge, and abolish the ignorance we are now spreading from our pulpit.

The European Protestants credited their values to teaching that evolved from the teachings of Martin Luther. Before then, the Catholic church had presented to the believers a doctrine of back doors, where an individual who might not be living quite to the Christian standard could still have an assurance of salvation by taking the sacrament and even in death the relatives could buy him out of hell and get him a place in heaven through indulgence.

That type of doctrine gives birth to a lifestyle of back doors, cutting corners, getting something for nothing. The consequence is that Europe went through a very bad period of her history, both politically and economically known as the Dark Age. There could be no development talk less of civilization in such circumstances. This is exactly the result our countries will have, if the church does not put an end to the spreading of ignorance and embrace knowledge, the truth of God's principles.

"There are no shortcuts to any place worth going." (Beverly Sills)

Europe was set free largely thanks to the Protestant reformation that began to teach that believers don't have any assurances to salvation through the back doors. According to the teachings of Martin Luther, John Calvin and their colleagues, sacraments do not get you salvation anymore and indulgence could not get your relatives out of hell fire. You now must live right and straight. This teaching from the Protestants made the believers to sit up and work out their salvation on a daily basis.

Then the Lord God took the man and put him in the Garden of Eden to tend and keep it.

Genesis 2:15

John Calvin and his teachings in Geneva played a decisive role in spreading this spirit of capitalism or protestant ethics. The cardinal point of his teaching, his doctrine of control by conscience, led to rigorous honesty in the daily lifestyle of the believers. John Calvin and his adherents taught that any form of waste must be frowned at, because people gave their lives to earn whatever they possess. This of course led to the view that luxury is a sin. The Calvinist did not believe in bringing all their money or worldly wealth to the church as the Catholics did. They were supposed to use it to do more good to their fellow men and the community.

These Protestants discouraged donation of money to the poor, because according to them, that could rather lead to beggary and laziness. According to them, a man is not supposed to be a burden to his fellow man. Neither should he be a nuisance to God by not working.

> **For even when we were with you, we commanded you this: if anyone will not work, neither shall he eat. For we hear that there are some who walk among you in a disorderly manner, not working at all, but are busybodies.**
>
> *2 Thessalonians 3:10-11*

In their teachings, when you fail to work you fail to glorify God. The preachers laid a huge emphasis on savings that could eventually lead to investments. That gave a huge boost to the development of new economy in Europe, banking, industrialization, etc. This led to mass productivity and production in the economy. Industrialization gave birth to wealth for an average man. Today however, most people are forced to work either for survival or to fulfill their greed for money, whereas the Protestants wanted to work to please God and to serve man.

These are the kind of teachings we must bring to our pulpits. We must stop spreading ignorance and erroneous teachings from our churches. Let's embrace this great knowledge of the principles of God from the early protestant Church. For only through knowledge can ignorance be eradicated. THE MOUNTAIN OF IGNORANCE! This mountain has to be leveled before we can have a transformation in our society.

THE CHURCH MUST ARISE TO HER PURPOSE AND PUT AND END TO THE SPREADING OF IGNORANCE!

NUGGETS
FROM CHAPTER 8

1. The church spreads Ignorance through erroneous teachings of ignorance from the pulpit.
2. The value system of the society is a direct result of the information the people in the society constantly feed on.
3. The church has contributed to the moral decadence of the society today.
4. The leaders of a nation are the products of the value system of that nation.
5. The church must put an end to the spreading of ignorance, by embracing the knowledge-able principles of God the Protestants lived by.
6. The protestant Church today should take a leaf from the early protestant church.
7. Life is 2% miracle and 98% principles.
8. Do not ask God to do for you, what he asked you to for yourself.
9. It is a sin not to work.
10. Don't seek miracles, seek principles and live by it.

CHAPTER 9

WHERE DID THE CHURCH MISS IT?

"All that is needed for the forces of evil to triumph is for enough good men to do nothing. All that is required for evil to prevail is for good men to do nothing. In order for 'evil' to prevail, all that need happen is for 'good' people to do nothing. All that is needed for evil to prevail is for good men to do nothing. The surest way for evil to prevail is for good men to do nothing. All it will take for evil to prevail is for good people to do nothing. All that is necessary for the forces of evil to take root in the world is for enough good men to do nothing. All that is needed for the forces of evil to succeed is for enough good men to remain silent. All it takes for Evil to prevail in this world is for enough good men to do nothing. The only thing necessary for the triumph of evil is for good men to do nothing."
(Edmund Burke)

It is indeed the fact and not just speculations that the church of the Lord Jesus Christ today has missed it big time in regards to the purpose that was in the heart of the Master for the church. The church has missed it in her teachings. The church has missed it in her doctrine.

The church has missed it in her ignorance of her purpose. The church has missed it in her lack of interest in the search of knowledge. The church has missed it in their silence to the evils in the society. Yes indeed the church has missed it! I couldn't agree any better with Edmund Burke. The only thing necessary for evil to prevail in our society today is for good men to do nothing. I strongly believe that good men (Christians) are not supposed to be silent at the evils perpetuated in the society today.

This is the one area where Christians have missed it big time. The church that was meant to be the voice of conscience to our societies, nations and world at large has gone into hiding, hiding in the four walls of the church. Separating her from the world, hiding from the very responsibility for which it was created. Hence the evils that has taken over our society today. Yet the church is still folding her hands and blaming the government for the problems of the society. The same church which is supposed to be the solution and answer to the problems in the society.

What has the church done? The church has left her purpose in pursuit of personal gain. The church has gone in pursuit of self-aggrandizement. Men of God have used the name of God in building empires for themselves. Subjecting people that meant to be saviors of the earth to servants in the four walls of the church. Hence the church has lost her glory. The church has lost her beauty. The church has lost her value. The church has lost her regard. The church has lost her respect. The church has lost her power in the society. The church has lost her influence in our nations. The church has really missed it!

To my shame, my nation and the church of the lord

Jesus Christ in my continent is covered head to toe in this ignorance. Ignorance could be said to be written in bold letters all over the institution that is supposed to be a shining light to the world. That is why I will not keep quiet until a revolution is started to fight ignorance and superstitions in the church of the Lord Jesus Christ and in the nation of my birth. This mountain must come down; the mountain of ignorance has to be brought down. The mountain of superstition has to be leveled for our people to taste a fresh breath of life in Christ Jesus.

WHAT IS THE CHURCH DOING WRONG?

What is the church doing wrong; some people might want to ask. I will like to give you a clear example to drive my point home. Take for example the last Nigerian general elections, after following the situation in our country carefully and the leadership that was in power, I discovered that if the country were to be left in the hand of the previous government for another four years that they were going to run the country down.

There were so many ills in the society, corruption has eaten deep into the fabric of the society and the president in charge seemed to be clueless as regard handling the situation in the nation. Nigeria as a nation was fast losing her credibility in the eyes of the international body. Yet our government seems not to care about the current situation in the country. The insecurity in the country was at its peak, insurgency, Boko Haram terrorism seemed to have been the order of the day. People dying here and there due to bomb blasts, yet our previous president seemed not to know the way, as matter of fact, he did not have any solution or a clear direction on the way forward for the country.

The church itself was ineffective in helping the situation in the country. All the church resulted to doing was praying. No one was taking any initiative as regards solutions to any of these problems in the nation. The best the churches resulted to was complaining and praying without taking any actions. To my amazement the church was about voting the same government into power again, with the excuse that he is a Christian president. That really gave me a deep thought of what Christianity in Nigeria has turned into. I could not help but kept asking myself the question who is a Christian?

- Is someone a Christian just because he was born in church?
- Is someone a Christian because he goes to church?
- Is someone a Christian because his parent goes to church?
- Is someone a Christian because his family members are all church people?
- Who exactly is a Christian?
- Is it possible for someone to be a Christian without possessing any values of Christianity?
- Is it possible to be a Christian without being Christ like?

These were all the questions going through my mind as I was listening to all these prominent ministers of the gospel promoting these misconceptions among the people. I could not help but see the level of the degradation of the church in my mother land. What I could see

182 ■ The Mountain Of Ignorance

in the churches in Nigeria was religious practice and a strong ignorance of what THE ROLE OF THE CHURCH IS SUPPOSED TO BE IN A NATION.

They came up with another speculation that Nigeria will be Islamized if the Muslim candidate became president of the country. Even though he was a better candidate with more integrity, they will rather go for the person without integrity because he calls himself a Christian. My question to this people was, since when did the salvation of a nation or people become dependent on who the president was? This whole situation surrounding the last Nigerian presidential elections only revealed to me how weak the church in Nigeria has become, how irrelevant the church has become to the society, how powerless the church has become. The church has lost her respect, because of people, individuals, churches and ministers that have no clue of what the church or Christianity is supposed to be.

In my despair I took to the Internet to speak up, and then I got to discover how far the church had fallen in value. My heart bleeds as I read the comments of "prominent ministers of the gospel" who I thought would have known better. The abuses from them on the Internet were as though these people had never been safe talk more of preaching the gospel. To my shame they actually believe they were doing what was right, to them they were defending the gospel. The insults, the abuses, the name calling were surprising; I was in a serious shock to know that such things could still come out of believers not just believers now but ministers. I could not help but cry out!

As if that was not enough, some said I should keep

quiet; they didn't want to hear what I had to say. I should tell them what God was saying. Even though God had told me who would win the election, I didn't want to come from that platform, I just wanted to engage their minds, getting them to think and see reasons why the previous government was not good enough for the nation. But no! My brethren would not think, they will not engage their faculties in reasoning, they just want to hear thus says the Lord. This is a serious form of ignorance. THE MOUNTAIN OF IGNORANCE!

Some even went to the extent of telling me about the different prophesies they had gotten from various ministers saying that the Christian president will win the elections which he lost anyways. This led me to discovering another big problem in the Nigerian church today which is SUPERSTITION. People are full of superstitions, they don't want to use their brains, and they don't want to take responsibility for their nation. It's rather safe for them to push their responsibility back to God. To an even greater astonishment, some were advising me to face my calling and leave politics alone. They said as a preacher I am not supposed to make my views known to the public, that I was partisan, others said I had backslidden; I was an agent of destruction, that I was bribed and all sorts of things, you cannot not even begin to imagine.

Among all these sayings the one that got to me most that really revealed the state of the Nigerian church, and not just the Nigerian church now, but the church worldwide was that I should FACE MY CALLING! What they meant by that, was preach the gospel that is what you were called to do. You have to concentrate on the pulpit, you can't comment on politics or the leadership in the country or the ills in the society. Pastor you have to remain in the four walls of the church.

REALLY!

- What then is my calling if I have to keep quiet at the face of the evil in the society?
- What then is the gospel, if not to spread light in the area of ignorance?
- The church seems to have forgotten that before Jesus died to save the world, there was a ministry He had. It was the ministry of light. Jesus came to shine light in every area of darkness in the world. He said I am the light of the world.

Then Jesus spoke to them again, saying, "I am the light of the world. He who follows Me shall not walk in darkness, but have the light of life.

John 8:12

The same Greek word used for light is used for knowledge and the same Greek word used for darkness is also used for ignorance. So Jesus came to eradicate ignorance from the earth, bringing knowledge in place of ignorance. This is the first calling every minister has. The ministry of light just like Jesus had the ministry of light while He was here on the earth. The church seems to be ignorant to this very truth. THE MOUNTAIN OF IGNORANCE! Ignorance has made the church to go into silence over the evils in our societies today. Yet we are complaining about them. This told me a lot about the state of the church today and where and how the church has missed it.

Ignorance is depriving the church of her purpose, value, influence, and respect in our society. It is so sad to admit this but this is the truth. The church is living in ignorance of her purpose. THE MOUNTAIN OF IGNO-RANCE! The church must rise back to her purpose and calling, the church must begin to live for the purpose for which it was established.

> *"The church must be reminded that it is not the master or the servant of the state, but rather the conscience of the state. It must be the guide and the critic of the state, and never its tool. If the church does not recapture its prophetic zeal, it will become an irrelevant social club without moral or spiritual authority. If the church does not participate actively in the struggle for peace and for economic and racial justice, it will forfeit the loyalty of millions and cause men everywhere to say that it has atrophied its will. But if the church will free itself from the shackles of a deadening status quo, and, recovering its great historic mission, will speak and act fearlessly and insistently in terms of justice and peace, it will enkindle the imagination of mankind and fire the souls of men, imbuing them with a glowing and ardent love for truth, justice, and peace. Men far and near will know the church as a great fellowship of love that provides light and bread for lonely travelers at midnight."*
> (Martin Luther King Jr.)

If the church does not retrace her steps we are at the verge of falling into the descriptions Martin Luther king Jr. made above.

DECEPTIONS IN THE CHURCH

Manipulation has become the order of the day in the church today. The church has been turned into a mini shrine. The church in Africa especially Nigeria has been turned into a place where people come to seek for the source of their problems. They want to know why they are not progressing, as every failure is ascribed or tied to a deity, or their great grandparents that do not want them to succeed or their enemies.

Bishops manipulating pastors, pastors manipulating leaders, leaders manipulating members and the circle goes on and on. Believers are now seekers of prophet instead of seekers of God. They are more interested in what the man of God will say to them instead of praying and seeking God for themselves. Their hearts have been sold out to deception and ignorance.

They are blinded by a strong desire for a quick solution and success without any desire for hard work. The church has succeeded in producing a bunch of needy miracle seekers in the church, People who only come to church to seek for solutions to their problems. Because they have forgotten the principles of Christ which says seek yea first the Kingdom of God and every other thing shall be added unto you.

But seek first the kingdom of God and His righteousness, and all these things shall be added to you.

Mathew 6:33

They have rather chosen to seek every other thing first except the kingdom. Hence they remain in perpetual need, irrespective of how much they seek their needs to be met; they remain needy slaves to their pastors "the slave masters". WHAT A MYTH! These people have become lovers of self instead of lovers of God. It is always about what they need, me, myself and I have become their favorite words. Is either: I need a Job, I need promotion, I need fruit of the womb (child), I need a husband/wife, I need a car, I need healing, I need deliverance for my family, I need more money. The list goes on and on, and endless list of needs.

Sadly this is their motivation for coming to church. Where their pastors had promised them that all their needs would be met, they don't need to work hard. All they need is God's favor in their life! One day of favor is worth more than a thousand years of labor, is their favorite saying. As much as this saying might be true, what they fail to explain to them is that this is not the principle on which life is meant to be lived. Miracle is just two percent of life and the remaining 98 percent is principles (hard work). These kinds of truth are not heard among them, neither is it welcomed. They are filled with the mindset of getting something for nothing. Forgetting that the bible has said he that does not work should not eat.

For even when we were with you, we commanded you this: If anyone will not work, neither shall he eat.

2 Thessalonians 3:10

ARE MINISTERS NOW GOD?

Ministers have exalted themselves to the place of God in the lives of their members. Dictatorship has become the order of the day. They have left the earth they were called to dominate to dominate humans. They have succeeded in raising a kingdom of slaves in churches instead of kingdom of sons. Their members are dependent on them. The common saying you hear among them is the man of God said this, the man of God said that, hardly will you hear from them what God said to them. Forgetting that the bible said as many as are led by the spirit of God are the sons of God. It didn't say those who are led by prophets or pastors.

For as many as are led by the Spirit of God, these are sons of God.

Romans 8:14

Please don't misunderstand me; I am not in any way against members asking for guidance or direction from their pastors or ministers. I am not against pastors advising their members. But what I am talking about here is pastors trying to play God in the lives of their members. One of my assistants told me a story of a particular pastor, a prominent minister who is very popular.

He said, one of this prominent minister's pastors came to him having heard from God concerning what God is asking him to do. He came to his pastor to share this vision with him, which he has been receiving from God consistently. God had instructed this young man to leave the church and start a movement that will reach out to the less privilege in the society and to be a voice to the poor. It was meant to be a non-governmental Organization NGO. That will reach out to these people both spiritually and physically. Every normal person would have thought the prominent minister of this young pastor will encourage him, but to my amazement that was not the case.

The minister went ahead and told this young pastor that he was not in the will of God. According to him, if it was God that was talking to him, God would have spoken to him first. Since God did not speak to him, automatically it means the brother did not hear from God. All the effort of this brother in trying to explain his series of visions from God concerning this issue fell on deaf ears. The pastor instructed him never to make mention of it again and he should concentrate on his service in the church. Stating that God cannot talk to this young pastor without first talking to him, which means God has to inform him first. In his words, "God does not work against spiritual authority". As shocking as this may sound the church leaders decided to put this brother on probation as according to them he is not submissive to spiritual authority, and as such should be used as an example so that others will learn from it.

If I understand perfectly well from this whole story, the minister's point is that God is supposed to talk to him first if it was genuine that God spoke to the young pastor. In other words God needed to take permission from him first before talking to this younger pastor about his vision. I really wonder where all these kinds of teaching is coming from in the body of Christ but let's continue with our story.

The brother having been told this, and after all the discouragement from his leaders, one would think he would stop but not for this brother. He was sure of what God told him to do, and he also had a great burden for it. So he decided to obey God. He left the church in search of how to fulfill his God given vision and purpose. The pastor took to the pulpit the next Sunday, declaring him A REBEL! Saying that he has left the covering, and the grace that their ministry has, has been removed from him. Therefore the only thing that awaits him is failure and calamities.

When I heard this story, my heart almost fell out of my chest. I could not help but ask, WHERE IS THE CHURCH GOING TO? WHAT HAS COME OVER THE PASTORS OF TODAY? WHAT BIBLE ARE WE READING? HOW DID WE FALL THIS FAR? So God now need to take permission from the men of God to speak to his children concerning the vision and purpose of their lives.

Another pastor stopped the marriage of a pastor under him to another sister claiming that it was not the will of God for the pastor, that if he got married to that lady he will have problem in his family. That God rather has revealed to him who his rightful wife is. That perfect will of God for this younger pastor was his own sister. This is someone he has no attraction whatsoever for. They are not compatible in anyway, he does not like her either. In conclusion, he left the church and got married to the love of his life and they have being living happily together for over 12 years now, they are blessed with four children.

These stories are stories of people that were bold enough to step out of the control of these so called men of God. Do you know how many more people have had their dreams crippled because of these pastors? This is to mention but a few…

ARE WE LOVERS OR KILLERS

One of my protégé's told me about a ministry that invited him to join their on-line program. One of the pastors from the ministry has told him about how wonderful the program was going to be and persuaded him to make out time to join the on-line program which he did. During the conclusion of the service the pastor said they were going to have a five-minute hot praise and that praise is to destroy kidnappers. That after the praise they were going to make some declarations that will kill any kidnapper that will make any attempt to kidnap any member of their commission (church).

I watched in wonder and amazement as the big congregation with thousands of people, sang whole heartedly and danced to the destruction of the kidnappers my protégé said. At the end of the praise the senior pastor (general overseer) took to the microphone and started this way. In his words "any person in this auditorium that will ask for mercy or forgiveness for any of these kidnappers is not a member of this commission (church) and is not supposed to be here so you can leave immediately. No one should ask for mercy for any kidnapper. Our declaration should be any kidnapper that was planning to kidnap any member of this commission will not see the breaking of tomorrow, they should die". He was watching the whole congregation declaring with all seriousness, shouting at the top of their voices that the kidnappers should die.

To add salt to the injury the pastor now said, there are people God kills by Himself, you have to kill them so you will be like your father. So when you get to heaven He will tell you well-done my child you are like me. At that point my heart almost fell out of my chest. I could not help but screamed out loud IS THAT A CHURCH OR A SHRINE!

The whole church seemed to be in agreement and in one spirit with the pastor as they all earnestly jumping up and shouting, and declaring the death warrant of the kidnappers. The big question is, what bible do this people read? Is it the same bible that said you should love your enemies and pray for those who despitefully use you? Or do they have a special bible for themselves?

But I say to you, love your enemies, bless those who curse you, do good to those who hate you, and pray for those who spitefully use you and persecute you, that you may be sons of your Father in heaven; for He makes His sun rise on the evil and on the good, and sends rain on the just and on the unjust.

Mathew 5:44-45

The second question that came to my mind is how has this kind of prayer been of any solution to the question of kidnapping in Nigeria? Is it really a fact that no member of that commission (church) has being kidnapped? And did the kidnappers die as they had prayed for? IGNORANCE HAS BECOME A MOUNTAIN INDEED IN THE BODY OF CHRIST.

Let's even say the prayers work, so what they mean by this their prayer is that the only people that the kidnappers cannot touch are people from their commission. If they try to kidnap people from their commission, the kidnappers will die, but it's OK if the people are not from their commission even though they are also Christians. Those ones could be kidnapped. If you don't want to be kidnapped come and join this commission. Well even though they didn't say this, these were just my thoughts as I heard this shocking story.

Instead of the church to seek for the solution to this problem in the society, they are declaring dead warrants. What I think a church will do is to organize programs for these youths, programs that will empower them and get them off the street in other to put an end or reduce these occurrences in the society to the nearest minimum. As a number of them are engaged in all these acts due to unemployment, poverty, lack and ignorance. But the church that is supposed to bring the light and solution to this problem of the society, is rather gathering to pray for the death of these young people they are meant to restore back to God. What an irony!

THE CHURCH HAS INDEED MISSED IT!

The church that was meant to provide solution to the ills of the society has lost focus of their purpose. I wonder why people continue in this kind of spiritual witchcrafts called prayer, even when they see it is not working and it is not providing a lasting solution. For every problem of the society the church is meant to device a means of solving each of them, providing a permanent solution to them all. Instead of the church being concerned about the possible solution of the problem we are facing in these area as a nation we are praying for the death of these people.

What amazes me is that some of the people praying this prayer did worse things before they got saved. What if God had killed them when they engaged in those evil activities before they got saved? The people they are praying for their death might be one of the wonderful talents the world is yet to know, that situation has pushed into acting in a way that was not God's original plan for them. Instead of the church devising a means on how to reach out to this people to get them saved and redirect them to who God has created them to be, the church is rather passing death sentence on them.

Did it for once occur to us that if God were to answer these kinds of prayers being prayed by these people it will actually be working for the kingdom of darkness by populating Hell and depopulating heaven. They will actually be acting like agents of darkness in this kind of mind set. Or it never occurred to us that any unrighteous person that dies unsaved is going to hell? How can believers be declaring death sentence on unbelievers that they are supposed to reach out to and win them in to the kingdom... This is ignorance in the highest order. THE MOUNTAIN OF IGNORANCE!

THE CHURCH IS TO BE SOLUTION ORIENTED

In my thinking, I would have thought that the church will raise people that will address this issue in the society. I would think that an NGO can be created that will do a thorough research on reasons why these young people engage in all these kinds of activities. Of which the reason is not far-fetched, this is a clear case of unemployment, idleness, poverty, etc.

My approach would be to start a movement that will address these causes, run trainings for the youths, empower them financially to be entrepreneurs thereby employing others, call the attention of the government and other well-meaning citizens that would be willing to sponsor some of these youths, minister to them both spiritually and physically. Spiritually, the work would be getting them saved and physically empowering them financially and thereby putting a permanent end to this evil in the society.

I believe this is what God expects from us. He has given the church the solution to the problem of the society. The bible said we are the light of the world; we are the salt of the earth. A city that is set on a hill cannot be hidden. It is high time the church pull down this mountain of ignorance that has made the church miss out on God's desire, will and purpose for the church. We have to rise up to our responsibility.

- The church is responsible for the safety of our society.
- The church is responsible for the wellbeing of her citizens.
- The church is responsible for the moral standard of a nation.
- The church is responsible for reaching out to the poor and needy of the society.
- The church is responsible for the orphans and struggling windows.
- The church is responsible for the rule of law in

the society.

- The church is responsible for justice in a nation.
- The church is responsible for upholding the moral values of the society.
- Yes it is the duty of the church to fight for the unity of her nation.
- God is counting on the church for the salvation of the nations and the earth at large.

For the earnest expectation of the creature waiteth for the manifestation of the sons of God.

Romans 8:19

For all creation groans and waits for the manifestation of the sons of God. It is our responsibility as believers to take care of the whole creature, and not just man. God is depending on the church, believers (you and I) for the restoration of the earth back to Himself. Let us arise to this responsibility. Until we do our nation and continent will remain in ruin. We are meant to be the light, the pace setters, and as such, we must arise to this responsibility in order to make our nation and the African continent great. The whole world is waiting for you and I. God is depending on us. WE MUST NOT FAIL GOD!

NUGGETS
FROM CHAPTER 9

1. The Church is meant to raise sons and not slaves.
2. The church is the answer to the problems in the society.
3. God is depending on the church for the restoration of the world.
4. As Christian and as a church, we must be solution oriented.
5. The church is the voice of conscience to the society.
6. The church is responsible for reaching out to the poor and needy in the society.
7. The church is responsible for the orphans and struggling windows.
8. The church is responsible for the rule of law in the society.
9. The church is responsible for justice in a nation.
10. The church is responsible for upholding the moral values of the society.

CHAPTER 10

HOW IGNORANCE IS DESTROYING THE CHURCH

"The more ignorant a man is the more he thinks he ought to govern someone else."
(Lewis F. Korns)

Indeed it is no secret that things are no longer the same in the church today. We cannot exactly say the church today is fulfilling the purpose for which it was created in totality. Like I said in the previous chapter the church has missed it. This negative shift in the church today is totally due to ignorance. Ignorance has become a mountain in the church today hence the destruction going on in the church. Ignorance has eaten deep down into the root of the church. It could be said, ignorance is flowing from the pulpit to the pew. Yes permit me to say that the church of today can be likened to what Jesus said throughout the gospels about the Pharisees and Sadducees.

The core values of the church are no longer known by the church of today. The beauty and dignity of the church seems to have lost its place in the society. The church has been turned to a place of entertainment rather than influence. The church is now a spectator to the happenings in the society. Why all these negative changes in the church? It is the destructive force of ignorance in operation.

WHAT GAVE THE EARLY CHURCH ITS BEAUTY?

This negative shift in the church today is totally due to ignorance. The church was proactive in providing solution to the problems of the society. The church did not separate herself from the society, but was rather very involved in its every spheres, hence their relevance. That is what the church of today has lost, RELEVANCE! There is no way the church can be relevant to the society if the church cannot provide solution to the problems of the society.

It is unfortunate that the churches of today are so self-centered that they cannot even see; talk less of providing solution to the problems of the society. If the church wants to be relevant, then the church must show her relevance by being a solution to the spiritual, physical, social needs of the society. The church must be a place that influences the society to uphold justice and morality of her citizens. Yes surely the negative shift in the church today is totally a factor of ignorance.

The modern civilization we are benefitting from today is thanks to the protestant Christians. Major evils in the postmodern society were stopped by Christians. It is not possible that such a solution-providing institution will not be relevant in the society. This is what the purpose and intension of God for the church is. The church was meant to be the light (solution) to the problem (darkness) of the society. All these evils in the society were stopped by Christians:

- The ending of slave trade in the western world
- The killing of twins in Africa

- The killing of female children (female infanticide) in China and India
- The burning of wife alive along with husband's dead body in Africa
- The establishment of civil right of the Black Americans etc.

THE EARLY CHRISTIAN CHURCH THROUGH THE MIDDLE AGES

Functional Contributions:

Rodney Stark (1997) has done an excellent analysis of how early Christianity arose and triumphed in the Roman world. Among the contributions he first noted was the Christian redefinition of disease. Many non-Christian religions defined disease as a result of a curse of God. This view was exemplified by the words of Jesus' disciples when they asked him what sin a blind man (or his parents) had committed (John 9:1-3). Jesus made it clear that disease was not necessarily the result of individual behavior, but rather just a part of living in the world. His healing ministry had an enormous impact on how his followers behaved.

Stark (1997) argues that Christians played a major role in changing how the Roman world not only defined illness but how the sick were treated. Matthew25:35-40 presents a final judgment motif not in terms of doctrine but in terms of social justice. This judgment story provided a strong impetus for Christian social action in the Roman world. There is evidence that early Christians, rather than abandoning the sick during epidemic periods, stayed in the community and cared for the sick.

They not only defined illness differently, but saw caring for the sick as sacerdotal (as making them holy) or at least following in the example of Christ. This resulted in what was to become a religious order of the hospitals (which cared for sick pilgrims) to the modern faith-based health care system. In fact, hôtel-Dieu, one of the old French terms for hospital, means "hostel of God" (Wikipedia, 2006). This attitude towards the sick and healing the sick dramatically changed Western culture in its fundamental attitude toward disease and how the sick were treated.

Many historians have noted the strong Christian contribution to learning. As the literate Roman world collapsed it was in the monasteries that the written word of God was kept as well as where the classics of the Greco-Roman world survived. It has been noted that much of this repository of written knowledge was hidden in Irish monasteries at the fringe of the conflict between the barbarians and the Romans. It was often the Celtic monks who reintroduced literacy into the new post Roman, Germanic world (Cahill 1996).

THE PROTESTANT REFORMATION

Some Functional Contributions:

Certainly since the work of Max Weber, entitled The Protestant Ethic and the Spirit of Capitalism (1930), sociologists have seen the Protestant reformation as a crucial event that contributed to redefining society. Weber argued that the capital formation which permitted industrial development characterized Protestant culture, emerging within the context of a work ethic that defined salvation itself dependent upon hard productive work, non-conspicuous consumption, and the production of goods and services that exceeded consumption.

Weber further argued that the focus on an individual judgment before God provided a sense of accountability that resulted in a strong civic attitude of contributing to the community and the needs of others (Shah & Woodberry, 2004). A variety of scholars have concluded that the Protestant reformation played a role in the development of democracy in Northern Europe as well as in other parts of the World.

The argument is that the idea of universal priesthood often (though not inevitably) results in universal suffrage in political democracies. In addition, if there is no Pope or Bishop how can there be a King (Hunt et al., 2000; Shah & Woodberry, 2004)? Shah and Woodberry further argued that the Protestant belief that every Christian must be able to read scripture provided a powerful impetus to universal education. Literacy, while not wide spread historically, is a fairly old cultural phenomenon.

What is unique about the concept of universal literacy is inherent in the term universal. They believe that not just an elite or specialized class needs to be literate, but that all need to be literate as a unique historical phenomenon that changed how human being thought and lived.

While early Protestant movements were often as intolerant as the medieval church, after periods of war between Protestants and Catholics and between various Protestant groups, a more tolerant pluralistic religion emerged. Some scholars believe (e.g. Hunt et al., 2000) that religious tolerance and pluralism related to wider acceptance of ethnic and cultural pluralism in general.

Both the Protestant Reformers and Catholic theologians in the Counter Reformation can be argued to have played a major role in the ending of slavery. Stark (2005) contends that such a perspective arises from a basic Christian view which is reflected in the U.S. Declaration of Independence: that human beings are endowed by the Creator with inalienable rights, which include liberty. As Stark noted (2005), by the 16th century Pope Paul III issued a Bill excommunicating those who traded or kept slaves.

The Protestant Countries of Northern Europe took similar civil action. In the United States, the first strong abolitionists were the Quakers, whose understanding of the New Testament and Pauline theology required equality. The influence of the Quakers moved many other religious groups, including the Puritan and Congregational traditions of New England, to provide a strong religious and moral base for the abolition of slavery (Ferrell, 2005).

Some sociologists, such as Stark in his recent work (2005), have argued that the dialectic between the Medieval Church, the Protestant Reformation and the subsequent Reform Movements in the Catholic Church have provided the very basis for rationalism, logic and general scientific advances in Western culture. The view that there was one God (a prime cause) and that both He and the nature He created could be understood by rational processes and deductive logic as well as by observation, exploration, and experiment, resulted in the significant progress of Western Societies.

204 ■ The Mountain Of Ignorance

THE CURRENT CHRISTIAN CHURCH IN A MODERN AND POST MODERN TIME

Even 2000 years after it began, the Christian church continues to have a significant impact on society. Christianity has grown to be the world's largest religion, with an estimated 2.1 billion members worldwide (Adherents, 2005), while over 76% of Americans report themselves to be Christians (Kosmin, Mayer, & Keysar, 2001).

This number represents all people who call themselves Christians, regardless of which church they claim membership with or even actual church membership in and of itself. In other words, in this postmodern world, from the perspective of many, one no longer needs to belong to a specific church or even any church in order to be called a Christian.

The focus of many Christian churches has begun to center on a blending of ideas and doctrines as well as a push towards new non- or inter-denominational churches that meet a wide variety of social and spiritual if not doctrinal needs (Hybels & Hybels, 1995). This ecumenism has in turn led to a seemingly greater tolerance of other beliefs and cultures in general society.

One of the recent emphases in society has been a move toward globalization. Globalization recognizes the interdependence of people around the world through the links of economics, politics, culture, and technology. It can be argued that Christianity has to a large extent driven this trend. Many Christian churches, engage in missionary activities, stemming from Jesus' command in the book of Matthew to "Go ye therefore and teach all nations".

The movement of missionaries and churches into countries and cultures previously unknown to the Western world has opened these countries up to movement in and out of ideas, customs, and material trade (Peterson etal. 2001). Given the universalism of the Christian Church, Peterson and associates argue that Christianity provided the basic underpinnings for globalization and the acceptance that all live in a global interconnected community.

Another impact of the Christian church on modern and postmodern society has occurred as a result of the church's strong focus on world relief, aid, and human as well as economic development. As mentioned earlier, this focus on humanitarian aid began with the early Christian Church in the care for the sick, and it continues till today.

Christian organizations, such as World Vision, Maranatha, and ADRA, have a significant impact on relief and aid around the world in areas such as medical services, AIDS care, community development, water purification, orphan services, economic aid, shelter, food provision, educational opportunities, as well as a host of other contributions (ADRA, 2005; World Vision, 2006; Evans, 1979).

These organizations are often some of the first major responders to disasters, as seen by the response to such catastrophes as the tsunami in East Asia and hurricanes in the United States. In addition to disaster response, organizations such as these operate full-time in many third world countries, and are continually changing societies around the world. Christian relief organizations have created a broader sense of responsibility throughout world governments, and have spawned other relief organizations, such as the Red Cross, in the public domain. One can readily notice that many of the changes to society which Christianity has caused have been related to Christianity's commitment to caring for others.

As Jesus said, one of the greatest commandments for Christians to follow is to "Love your neighbor as yourself". This statement, as well as the story of the Good Samaritan that it precedes, invokes a responsibility that has not only led to the creation of world aid and relief organizations, but also to several very large hospital systems. The role of health care provision during the rise of the Christian church has been noted, but that role continues to this day. A large proportion of hospitals today in the United States are nonprofit organizations with religious affiliations (FTC & DOJ, 2004).

Although today there are also many for-profit as well as government-run hospitals, the system of health care that we have today was started and maintained by Christians in an effort to better serve God and humanity. Christianity also had a major effect in the civil rights movement in the mid to late 20th century. In the 1950s and 60s, protests against the denial of civil rights and liberties to African Americans became a large controversy in the United States.

Many Christian churches took a strong stand on the side of granting civil rights, backed by Paul's statement in Galatians that "There is neither Jew nor Greek, slave nor free, male nor female, for you are all one in Christ Jesus" (Gal. 3:28, NIV). Many of the leaders in the civil rights movement came from among Christian pastors, including Dr. Martin Luther King Jr. and Rev. Ralph

Abernathy. One of the largest civil rights organizations at the time, the Southern Christian Leadership Conference, was created, governed, and operated by Christian leaders. This organization was often at the forefront of the movement, organizing events such as the 1965 Selma to Montgomery Freedom March, and was involved in the 1963 March on Washington for Jobs and Freedom, where Dr. King delivered his famous speech. Religious influence can be seen in his claim on rights from the standpoint of demanding justice for "all of God's children" (King, 1963) and the quotation of multiple Bible verses.

In addition to providing leaders and support for the civil rights movement, Christianity was influential in the nature of the movement and its conductance. The U.S. civil right movement mostly upheld the early Christian ideals of peace, non-combatant, and pacifism (see first section of paper). Many parts of the civil rights movement were centered on these ideas, creating a nonviolent movement focusing on civil disobedience and peaceful demonstrations, leading to a major change in civil rights and liberties, including affirmative action, civil rights acts, voting rights acts, and desegregation.

These and many others, too numerous to mention here, are the various achievement of Christianity. One might want to say how then, can you say ignorance is destroying the Church after all the said achievements of Christian works and movements.

Well that is where the major issue is, in as much as there is no doubt to the achievement of the church today, I like to greatly differ in my perspective as regards this. In that most of the accomplishment of the church have been centralized around the meeting of the direct needs of the people. This is not in any way bad, of course it is very expedient that we do this. But the problem is that it has made the church to be more conscious of self: what I can get, what the church is supposed to do for me, what I want to get from God than being kingdom conscious. Many people who are actually involved in charity today do not necessarily do it because of the love they have for people but rather because of what they can get from it. Sad enough this situation is found in our churches today. This is nothing more than ignorance in operation.

The church has been ignorant of the full Gospel Jesus Christ came to preach and commanded us to preach. This is the major course or root through which ignorance is destroying the church. Like a popular saying goes "half-truth is as bad as or even worse than no truth".

WHAT GOSPEL DO YOU PREACH

Largely today, the only gospel that is popular in the body of Christ is the gospel of salvation. This still centers on I and you, I want to be saved, you have to be saved, Jesus saved me, and Jesus saved you. You can now claim the benefits that come with salvation, because you are saved. Is there anything wrong with this? Someone might want to ask. My answer is no, but after you are saved, what next? This is where the major problem of the church is, it is in the gospel we preach.

If you read through the four gospels (Mathew, Mark, Luke and John) you will not find where Jesus was preaching to the crowd the gospel of salvation. It was always the gospel of the kingdom. The gospel of the kingdom is the gospel Jesus left for the church to preach.

The gospel of the kingdom is the gospel that transforms the society. It is the gospel of the kingdom that goes beyond personal needs to national needs. The gospel of the kingdom cannot be silent or indifferent to the ills in the society. The gospel of the kingdom gives rise to national transformation. The gospel of the kingdom is the complete gospel.

It is the absence of the gospel of the kingdom in our pulpits that has resulted in the nominal and passive Christianity we have today. Christians that feel that being tolerant to the evils of the society is equivalent to loving people. What ignorance! Ignorance indeed has become a mountain in Christendom and if the church must fulfill her purpose on the earth, this mountain has to be pulled down.

Take for example what is happening in the United States of America today. First it was the removal of bible from schools, then the stopping of prayers in schools, making abortion legal, now the legalization of gay marriage in a country that claims to have 76% of its population to be Christians. What kind of Christians do we have today? Yet to make matters worse many of these Christians don't seem to see anything wrong with all these happenings in their society. Those who claim to see something wrong about it only complain. And those who even talk against it are labeled to be judging the people, including some of the Christians.

I earlier told you about how I heard of a famous preacher in America who said in his interview, concerning the gay marriage that, "the Church will always be the Church and the world will always be the world". That statement tore me apart. I was amazingly astonished at the kind of ovation and clapping he was receiving at the end of his speech. This really broke my heart. It only exposed me to the level at which ignorance is destroying the body of Christ. The body of Christ seems not to know what it stands for anymore. Whoever told us that we have to be tolerant to the perpetration of evil in the society in order to show that we love people? What is this level of degradation all about? Is it the fact that we are seeking to be accepted by the society? Or we are seeking to be famous?

I could not help but wonder how Jesus will be disappointed at us. It is time the Church arises from where she has fallen. The church in America needs to wake up to the realities facing them, for if the church does not wake up and put an end to this ignominy in America, I'm sorry to say that there will be no future for America as a nation. The Church has failed in her responsibility to the society. We have failed to stand up for what is right. We have failed to voice out against moral decadence in the society. We have failed to stand up against injustice. Yes we have failed!

The church has rather ran back to the four walls of a building, with no influence whatsoever in our society. My heart bleeds! I am totally disappointed by the happenings in the body of Christ today. All we are concerned about is the size of our congregation, the size of tithe and offerings in the church. How popular we are in the society. How famous our congregation is in the society. The church has been destroyed by ignorance and self-aggrandizement. We have to put an end to the various vices in the society. THE CHURCH IS THE ONLY HOPE OF THE SOCIETY! As long as we are willing, all things are possible. And yes the Church can be relevant again. We have to restore the beauty of the church back. We have to embrace knowledge and stand up for our responsibility in our society.

The Nigerian church must take responsibility for every problem in our society. We must be solution providers. We have to acquire the necessary knowledge required to change our nation for the better, our continent and the world at large. We must begin movements that will encourage the mass to seek knowledge and be educated. We are the only hope for a better Nigeria and the continent of African.

Dear reader, we have come to the end of part two. You are welcome to the last part of this book (part 3) and my very best part too. In the first chapter in this part, I will be discussing the topic "why is this my business" Stay with me, lets enjoy this last part together.

NUGGETS
FROM CHAPTER 10

1. The gospel Christ preached is the gospel of the kingdom.
2. The gospel of the kingdom is the complete gospel.
3. The church is not meant to be indifferent to the vices in the society.
4. Silence to evil is not equivalent to love.
5. This negative shift in the church today is totally due to ignorance.
6. All these evils in the society where stopped by Christians:
   - The ending of slave trade in the western world.
   - The killing of twins in Africa.
   - The killing female children (female infanticide) in china and India.
   - The burning of wife alive along with husband dead body in Africa.
   - The establishment of civil right of the Black Americans etc.
7. It is the absence of the Gospel of the kingdom on our pulpits that has resulted to the nominal and passive Christianity we have today.

8. The early church contributed greatly to the civilization we have today. Even most modern technologies were discovered by Christians. The modern day hospital we have today is thanks to the early Christians.

PART 3

THE DIRE CONSEQUENCES OF IGNORANCE

CHAPTER 11
·····························
WHY IS THIS MY BUSINESS?

"If any earthly institution or custom conflicts with God's will, it is your Christian duty to oppose it. You must never allow the transitory, evanescent demands of man-made institutions to take precedence over the eternal demands of the Almighty God."
(Martin Luther King, Jr.)

Why is this my business? Well, my special answer to this question is always the same. It is my business because it is God's business. And it should be every believer's business, because we are God's representatives on the earth. Oh yea, it is my business! It is not just my business, it is my calling. I am following in the footsteps of my Master Jesus Christ; He came and declared in John 8:12 "I AM THE LIGHT OF THE WORLD" (τὸ φῶς "The light" is from phos, which means both "light" and is the metaphor for "knowledge.").

Light in Greek is also used as a metaphor for knowledge which is the opposite of ignorance. He came to the earth as the Light of the world because the whole world lies in darkness. Someone must stand up to confront and dissipate darkness. Hence, the creator of the universe sent His only begotten Son to the earth so that through the power of light he would destroy darkness which is ignorance.

It is that same ministry that I have been called to.

I believe every minister of the gospel is called to this ministry first of all. The ministry of light, the ministry of destruction of darkness, the ministry of setting people free from ignorance. Light is what we are called to preach. Our Lord and Savior called Himself the Light of the world. If we preach Him, it means we preach light. Consequently we preach freedom from ignorance.

Most times when we talk about Jesus, we talk about Him only as the Savior of the world, but before He died to save the world, He had a ministry and that ministry was about eliminating ignorance (darkness) and all its consequences of destructions, calamities and sorrows in the world.

I therefore beg to disagree with people who say that I am diverting from my main ministry when I write or talk about the different areas of ignorance and problems in the society. No, no, no, no, Sir! I am in the mainstream of my calling by writing on politics in Nigeria, in Africa, in the church and the world at large. I am being a minister of light and a destroyer of ignorance and I shall never keep quiet until this horrendous mountain is pulled down in my country, in the church of Christ, in my continent and in the world at large.

Often times when I speak up against the evils in the society, I hear things like, "is it your business? You like trouble". Believers telling me to face my calling, and most times I just get amazed at all these comments. The understanding of believers today as regards our responsibility to our society is rather alarming, I must say. The only clear reason I can say is the cause of these kind of response is Ignorance! THE MOUNTAIN OF IGNORANCE! And this mountain must be pulled down for us to have a breath of fresh air.

What I wish to let my fellow Christians know in this chapter of the book, is that whatsoever God will not keep quiet to, we have no right as believers to be quiet to such things. As true ambassadors of Christ, we must learn to represent Christ rightly. We must always stand against the evils in the society. Anytime you find yourself in a situation where you just want to be quiet against the ills of the society to avoid trouble, or name-calling, ask yourself this simple question; "what will Jesus do if He were to be in my shoe?"

Let the answer to that question determine what you do in such situations. We have to be conscious of the fact that we are the extended hands of Jesus on the earth. We must learn to lend our voice to Christ through speaking up when necessary. Being silent when you are meant to speak is being a coward and a hypocrite. It is your sole duty and my duty, to take responsibility for the happenings in our societies. Until we learn to take personal responsibility for the happenings in our society, we can't get the change we are so much anticipating for.

PERSONAL RESPONSIBILITY

Have you ever been in the company of people, who will complain about how their country is not working, how the politicians are the problem in their nation, how the government is not doing things rightly, complaining of why the nation is not working, how the world is coming to an end, how America is falling, how Christians have failed etc. blaming everything and everyone else, except themselves the righteous ones. Hey! Could that person be you?

I personally had fallen victim to this line of reasoning for a considerable amount of time in my life. As years go by though, I discovered that as in many other things, I had simply fallen victim of my environment. I saw people around me blame the nation and everything else that is wrong in the country, on one person or the other and I simply joined them. I heard them talk about it, I witnessed them playing the blame game, and I joined them, on and on it went. The vicious cycle of the blame game at times seems to be very sweet as the complainer; it seems to make you the only righteous one who can see everything that is wrong about the society.

> **When I was a child, I spoke as a child, I understood as a child, I thought as a child; but when I became a man, I put away childish things.**
>
> *1 Cor 13:11*

However thank God for knowledge, thank God for understanding, thank God for insight, thank God for education. After getting myself relatively educated in the area of national transformation, I have come to discover that it makes better sense to look at what I could do to fix the problem of the society, rather than blaming others for what is wrong in the country.

As a matter of fact I never seriously thought about the word responsibility until I was doing my masters in the university. I was fortunate to listen to a man address the issue of men's responsibility. The word seemed so common and popular that I never thought it needed much attention, but the more I studied it the more I discovered, hey! Wait a minute; I never really knew anything about the true meaning of the word. At least my life style did not show any form of responsibility for the nation where I was born or the nation where I lived.

Today, I can joyfully say that one of the best undertakings I have ever made was to study the subject of responsibility. As obvious as my assertion in this article is, so many people still don't think very seriously about the fact that personal responsibility is one of the most essential credentials in national transformation.

The now famous and widely used quotation of John F. Kennedy

> *"Ask not what your country can do for you;*
> *ask what you can do for your country"*

is probably the most circulated quotation on the subject of personal responsibility of a citizen towards his nation. If a nation and any nation for that matter can raise up the standard of personal responsibility in their society, you will in no time see a country of virtuous people, developed and civilized.

> *"The price of greatness is responsibility."*
> *(Winston S. Churchill)*

If you are reading this book, I like to believe that you must be interested in the transformation of your society, nation and the world at large. If that is the case then you must start with yourself. The most obvious question of a responsible person is what can I do in this situation? The more we can ask such questions, the more we bring about change where we are. Instead of expecting someone from somewhere to spearhead or bring about a change that we desire, it is much more practical to begin to do something personally.

> "*Most people do not really want freedom, because freedom involves responsibility, and most people are frightened of responsibility.*"
> (Sigmund Freud)

A responsible citizen is the one that sees something wrong in the society, something he is not satisfied with or that he cannot agree with and responds not by blaming the government or leaders; but by designing ways and means of bringing a lasting solution to the issues at hand.

THE TRUTH

For a nation to be truly transformed there must be movements, civil societies, NGOs etc. that are spread all across the land to educate people on the issues of personal responsibility. If a nation or rather active citizens of a nation could successfully launch such campaigns and a good percentage of the populace begin to live by the principles of personal responsibility, which is "don't blame others", think of what you can do to fix it. Such a nation would cross the hurdle of civilization in a record time.

Dear reader, are you going to begin with yourself by responding rather creatively to the issues you see around your nation? It is easier to say that there is no way I could personally address every single problem in my nation, they are too many. Oh yea, you cannot fix all problems, but you can fix some problems, more importantly you could bring enlightenment to all others around you.

"Choices may be unbelievably hard, but they're never impossible. To say you have no choice is to release yourself from responsibility and that's not how a person with integrity acts."
(Patrick Ness)

If each one, in your area of influence, would offer to do at least something about what they have a burden for, soon everybody in the nation would be doing something leading to a massive movement of enterprises, entrepreneurship, services, charities, etc.

The truth is that everyone, if he is human must be aware of his own responsibility for himself, for others, for all and for something. That is a part of what makes us human. This is because we are created to become a solution to some needs or the other in the world. We are all here to make our world a better place. If you would not take action and responsibility for those things you were created for, that does not mean you escape the responsibility, you still face that responsibility one way or the other. Unfortunately this realization often comes in form of regret, pain and sorrow.

"Eventually we all have to accept full and total responsibility for our actions, everything we have done, and have not done."
(Hubert Selby Jr.)

There is nothing more important in life, no greater factor to success than personal responsibility. Until individuals begin to take personal responsibility for the situations in the society, there will be little or no visible change.

As Christians, one of our duties which I call our responsibility is to be the voice, or the conscience of the society. We have to speak up for moral uprightness in the society. We have to fight for justice to the poor, needy and less privilege. We have to ensure the rule of justice in the society at large. To be indifferent to the problems in the society is ignorant. It is only ignorance that makes us feel, oh there is no need to talk about that, after all its not affecting me or any member my family.

Believe it or not, a time is coming when the things you have refused to speak up for will begin to chase you, your children, friend, or a family member, be it directly or indirectly. That is just the truth about life. When we become indifferent to the evil in the society, we are encouraging darkness to supersede light in our society. We live in ignorance that way, THE MOUNTAIN OF IGNORANCE!

THE SIN OF IRRESPONSIBILITY

God created the world and everything in it belongs to Him. Everything we have was given to us by the Lord. Even the life we have was given to us by Him on rent. We are totally dependent on God and we owe Him our lives, because He can take it away at any time. God gave us the life we are living on rent, so He has every right to charge us for it. The only payment God desires from us is fruitfulness. Our lives must bring benefit to the Creator and to people, thereby responding to God's love and trust.

Do you remember how Jesus answered the question about paying taxes? He said you have to pay not only to the government but also to God, "They say unto him, Caesar's. Then He said to them: Render therefore to

Caesar what is Caesar's and unto God what is God's" (Matt. 22:21). As every citizen is required to pay national taxes, so each person will be required to report to God for his life on earth.

God created the beautiful planet and created all the conditions for mankind to live. Just like the master, who planted a vineyard for tenants, God the Father has prepared a land for us. He prepared everything for us to enjoy life; He created trees to breathe fresh air and eat of their fruit, He entrusted to us immense natural resources, and so much more.

The Lord took care of our needs and has the right to expect fruit from us. We need to take responsibility for the life God gave us, for the blessings and talents He gave us and for the world He committed to us. Therefore keeping silent to the ills in the society is a sin to both man and God. It is the sin of irresponsibility. Irresponsibility always comes with a high price tag. Can you say for certain that your life brings forth fruit to God and humanity or have you been living for yourself? Your answer will determine what role you will play in the history of mankind.

Are you living a life of irresponsibility? Have you been committing the sin of irresponsibility while thinking you were facing your calling? Even though we were not responsible people before our salvation, after we receive Christ we should begin to take full responsibility for our society and the people, for God to bless the works of our hands. Before God can trust us with something He has to be sure that we will take responsibility of what He trusts us with. God does not have any business with irresponsible people. He cannot trust His treasures into their hands. He only trusts those who have proven themselves to be trustworthy (responsible).

THE PRICE AND PAIN OF IRRESPONSIBILITY

There is always a great price to pay for irresponsibility. Be it irresponsibility to self, family, society or nation. You might either pay this painful price directly or indirectly. The bottom line is there is always a high price tag that comes with irresponsibility. You pay this price irrespective of your choice. It doesn't matter if you want to pay or not. It is automatic.

> *"You cannot escape the responsibility of tomorrow by evading it today."*
> (Abraham Lincoln)

An example that comes to mind is a situation where we refuse to pay attention to the less fortunate people in our neighborhoods. If every single person in the elite of our society will take care of at least one child, most of the street kids would be taken care of. Yet, we act as if it is none of our business.

Truly in the short term, there tends to be no consequences to our act of irresponsibility. However in the long run most of those kids are now grown-ups and are the fearful nocturnal visitors with weapons attacking the same neighborhood, raping our daughters and wives, maiming our sons and husbands, turning our lives into a nightmare. Our response is another blame game. We turn our attention to the government and we whine about the incompetence of the police, we also complain about the breakdown in law and order. Yet, we forget that we actually had a role to play in the consequences we are reaping.

When we refuse to do what we are supposed to do at the right time, the consequence is that of pain and tragedy. When a people refuse to pay the price of personal responsibility for the problems of the nation, these same people end up paying the high price of irresponsibility, which is often in tragedy and sorrow.

We often blame our government for their lack of responsibility, socially and politically. We forget about the fact that it is only a result of the societal irresponsibility in general. When there is no personal responsibility in any society, there cannot be a responsible government. Responsible government is an off shoot of a culture of personal responsibility. As you and I take personal responsibility for mending the things that are out of order in our community and nation in general, we would surely witness a transformed, developed and civilized society. Therefore it should be my and your business to bring solutions to the problems in our society.

IF IT IS JESUS BUSINESS IT'S MY BUSINESS

For sure if it is Jesus' business then it is my business. What other business do I have, if is not the business Jesus gave me on the earth? What other part can be followed except for the part and examples Jesus left behind? I like you not to forget the very point we started from that lead us to where we are now. WHY IS THIS MY BUSINESS?

Dear readers, each time you are faced with a situation that you are tempted to be indifferent to, like I said earlier, ask yourself this question; what will Jesus do in this situation? The sincere answer to that question should determine your next line of actions. Jesus was never indifferent to the needs of people, society and nation. He was not indifferent to the corrupt practices among the scribes, Pharisees and Sadducees. Jesus spoke to the general need of the people and nation at large. He spoke up for the justice of the oppressed. A perfect example is in the case of the woman that was caught in the act of adultery.

But Jesus went to the Mount of Olives. Now early in the morning He came again into the temple, and all the people came to Him; and He sat down and taught them. Then the scribes and Pharisees brought to Him a woman caught in adultery. And when they had set her in the midst, they said to Him, "Teacher, this woman was caught[b] in adultery, in the very act. Now Moses, in the law, commanded us that such should be stoned. But what do You say?" This they said, testing Him, that they might have something of which to accuse Him. But Jesus stooped down and wrote on the ground with His finger, as though He did not hear. So when they continued asking Him, He raised Himself up[g] and said to them, "He who is without sin among you, let him throw a stone at her first." And again He stooped down and wrote on the ground. Then those who heard it, being convicted by their conscience, went out one by one, beginning

with the oldest even to the last. And Jesus was left alone, and the woman standing in the midst. When Jesus had raised Himself up and saw no one but the woman, He said to her, "Woman, where are those accusers of yours? Has no one condemned you?" She said, "No one, Lord." And Jesus said to her, "Neither do I condemn you; go and sin no more."

John 8:1-11

Jesus Christ was never indifferent to injustices, needs, problems and troubles of the people throughout His stay on the earth. He always attended to every need, irrespective of who is involved. Jesus went about doing good and healing all that were sick. As representatives of Christ on the earth, as His ambassadors, we are supposed to follow His footsteps. We are to borrow a leaf from Christ our Master.

Everything in the society that is wrong is our responsibility to fix. As Christians, we have to work on our societies; we have to live in the consciousness of reproducing the kingdom of God on the earth. We have to know that God is depending on us for the salvation of nations not just individuals. We are the ones to bring salvation and restoration to the earth.

For the earnest expectation of the creation eagerly waits for the revealing of the sons of God. For the creation was subjected to futility, not willingly, but because of Him who subjected it in hope; because the creation itself also will be delivered from the bondage

of corruption into the glorious liberty of the children of God.

Romans 8:19-21

Always live in the consciousness of the fact that God sent you to the earth to fix the problems on the earth. This was what Jesus did; He lived His whole life for it, even in death, He died for people and the earth at large. The shoes Jesus left behind are big ones to step in. We must brace ourselves up for this great task. Jesus Christ was a people person His whole life, He lived and died for people. Until we begin to live for people and stop living for self, we have not started living, we just exist.

It is therefore my business and your business to proffer solution to the problems in the society. The difficulties of people should be our business. It is our business to restore the earth back to God through the principles of the Kingdom. We therefore need to arise to the task and take personal responsibility for the peace, growth, development of our people and our nations.

If Nigeria will change for the better, then we must take responsibility for the changes in Nigeria. We must stop expecting the government to play the role of national transformation why we sit down and watch. Every individual has a role to play for the betterment of our nation. The African continent must arise and fight to restore her beauty and bring solution to her problems. We the people are the solutions we seek. It is time to make Nigeria and the African continent great. Arise o compatriots!

NUGGETS
FROM CHAPTER 11

1. It is our business to proffer solution to the problem of the society.
2. We cannot be indifferent to the evil in our society.
3. We have to lend our voice to Christ by speaking on His behalf.
4. Jesus was never indifferent to the issues of the people in His day.
5. Jesus had the ministry of light (knowledge).
6. We have to confront ignorance in our nation.
7. If it is God's business then it should be your business.
8. Personal responsibility leads to national transformation.
9. Irresponsibility is a sin with a high price tag.
10. God has no business with irresponsible people.

CHAPTER 12

SATAN RULES THROUGH DARKNESS, GOD RULES THROUGH LIGHT

"Light always overcomes darkness."
(Donald L. Hicks)

Then Jesus spoke to them again, saying, "I am the light of the world. He who follows Me shall not walk in darkness, but have the light of life.

John 8:12

From the previous chapters, I have mentioned that the same word used for light in Greek is also used for knowledge, and the same world used for darkness, is also used for ignorance. (τὸ φῶς "The light" is from phos, which means both "light" and is the metaphor for "knowledge. τῇ σκοτίᾳ, "Darkness" is skotia, which means both "darkness" and is the metaphor for "ignorance."). If we are going to relate this to the topic at hand, it will be said that God rules through Knowledge and satan rules through ignorance.

It is no doubt that the only area of strength for Satan's ruler-ship is in our area of ignorance. He takes advantage of people especially believers in their area of ignorance. If there is anything the devil will want to keep you from having, it is knowledge. The devil will do anything for you to be comfortable in your ignorance. Why? Because his strength can only be perfected in your area of ignorance (darkness), Ignorance is therefore a very useful weapon in the hands of the devil against humanity, especially Christians. It is quite unfortunate that believers today give the devil an upper hand in their life affairs by allowing ignorance to reign in their lives. THE MOUNTAIN OF IGNORANCE!

When we neglect knowledge, we have indirectly rejected light. We most times want to be and live in our comfort zone; we therefore feel that it is expensive or difficult to pursue knowledge. Then we settle for what seems to be easy for us, which is ignorance because ignorance seems to be much easier and less expensive at the moment. But the price of ignorance is way more than the price we would have paid to acquire knowledge. The price of ignorance is usually a life of frustration and destruction.

> *"If you think education is expensive, try ignorance."* *(Derek Bok)*

Joe was a high school student who felt that it was too difficult to wake up every morning to go to school, having classes and all the assignments he had to do every day. So he decided that he was not going to continue into tertiary institution the moment he was done with his high school.

Despite the parents' persuasion for him to go to tertiary institution he refused, it was as though all their advice fell on deaf ears. He rather took a job as a sales person to a newspaper company located on his street where he lived. He became comfortable because of the salary he was receiving.

The younger sibling Dave finished high school and went to tertiary institution where he majored in business management. Today Dave has his own company and several businesses. Meanwhile Joe is still struggling to make ends meet, living on pay check to pay check. He could hardly meet his primary needs and that of his family.

Joe's greatest regret today is if only I had known I would have listen to my parents. I would have continued my education. I would have paid the price for a better future. This is what ignorance does to us. When we think it is difficult to pay the price of getting knowledge, then we end up paying the highest price for our ignorance. The end result is always a life of regret and pain. Do not let the temporal pain of discipline you need to acquire knowledge stop you from acquiring it. If you do, you will live your life time in perpetual pain of regrets and limitations in life.

WHAT IS IT THAT DESTROYS US

If you were giving the opportunity to answer this question, I am sure you will have a full list of the things you think are the reasons for the destruction of humans or people. Some will say oh for sure, the devil is the number one reason for all destructions, witches and wizards, poor economy, war, bad government and politicians, unemployment, poverty, etc. But let it be known to you that none of those things you have in mind are the true reasons for destruction. Some people say, "the government and politicians are not doing their due diligence they are destroying the masses. The devil is the reason for all the problems we have in the society. How can you say otherwise?"

Well, as relevant as some of those claims above might seem to you, I beg to disagree with you my dear readers. What! Pastor Sunday, What are you trying to say? Are you in any way insinuating that the devil is not responsible for the destructions in our life and society? Are you trying to defend the government and politicians? What exactly are you saying? Is it not so obvious to you that these are the major problems we are having in our society and hence the destructions.

I know it is always very convenient to shift the course of our problems to others and to the devil especially common among religious people. But that is just a mere speculation, sorry to say, yea I am sorry if I am messing with your religious mind and beliefs right now, but that is the truth. The only thing destroying us is ignorance! (Darkness) THE MOUNTAIN OF IGNORANCE! Even the devil has no power over us except in our area of ignorance. Let's stop glorifying the devil, giving him power that he does not deserve or have.

We are the author of our own destruction. We destroy ourselves when we are ignorant or decide to live in ignorance. Because we are lazy or too comfortable to step out of our comfort zones to seek knowledge. Yes! When we live in ignorance, we live in darkness and that is where the devil rules. You cannot be stronger than a king of a territory. As long as you want to live in the territory of the devil, the territory of ignorance (darkness) he will destroy you because that is his area of speciality. But when you step out into light (knowledge) where God rules you become a danger to him; too dangerous for him to handle. You dismantle; strip him of every power he thought he had over you.

> *"Knowledge will forever govern ignorance; and a people who mean to be their own governors must arm themselves with the power which knowledge gives."* (James Madison)

We are the ones that give power to the devil to destroy us by living in darkness (ignorance). Yes for sure the devil rules in darkness. And we will be doing a great harm to ourselves to live in darkness (ignorance), which is by itself a great harm. Nothing in the whole world is more dangerous than ignorance (darkness). Every evil we see in our society today can be traced back to ignorance.

> *"An ignorant person is, by the very fact of his or her ignorance, a very dangerous person."* (Hendrik W. Van Loon)

There is no difference between the person living in ignorance and the person living in darkness. So to break yourself loose from the dominion, ruler-ship and manipulation of the devil, you have to embrace light (knowledge). Light always overshadows and out powers darkness. Darkness is subject to light, and can never manifest itself in the presence of light. That is why it is appalling to me, to see why believers who are children of light being afraid of darkness, or living in subjection to it. This is an abnormality and should be corrected immediately. The only way it can be corrected though, is by you embracing the light (knowledge). Seeking knowledge with all passion within and therefore moving out of ignorance (darkness).

The only reason for your intimidation by the devil, and your being afraid of him, or what he can do is because you are living in ignorance (darkness) which is his territory. The only power he has over you is the power you give to him through ignorance of your position as a child of light. It is time to put an end to the ruler-ship of darkness, ignorance, THE MOUNTAIN OF IGNO-RANCE! And embrace the light by making a conscious effort to pay the price of living in the light, which is seeking knowledge in every area of our lives.

God indeed rules through light. Satan rules through darkness. As children of light, it is therefore an insult to live in the fear of darkness; when you have been given authority over darkness. Light does not need to struggle with darkness, the moment you turn on light, darkness bows without any negotiation. You don't need to argue, you don't need to go on fasting and prayer, and you don't even need to pray before handling darkness. All you need to do is turn on the light. The moment you turn on the light, no matter how thick that darkness was, it disappears automatically. It bows! Darkness has no choice but to bow before light.

For you to be able to turn on the light in the darkness though, you have to live in the light. As just claiming I am a child of light is not going to get the job done. To say it in another way is like just claiming I have knowledge of a thing without studying or doing my due diligence to really get to have the knowledge. That I just claimed it, said it, professed it, is not going to give me the knowledge I need.

If I must have the knowledge (light), I must pay the price of getting it, which is; studies, research, and hard work. Only then can I really have it, and be able to use it against darkness. As long as you are ready to pay this price for living in the light (knowledge) the darkness (ignorance) becomes a servant to you. You become a threat to darkness and not the other way round.

On the other hand, if you are not ready to pay the little price of living in the light (knowledge) then you will automatically pay the great price of living in darkness (ignorance) where the devil will be your boss and master, thereby making yourself open to the destructive force of ignorance, THE MOUNTAIN OF IGNORANCE! It is only in this situation that you will be susceptible to the destructive force of the devil.

So you see, satan has no right over you, the devil has no power over you, except in the area of your ignorance where you have given him the right to do so. You therefore are the cause of your destruction; your ignorance is the cause of your destruction. The devil cannot destroy you when you live in the light (knowledge). We should therefore not pay too much attention to him; you should rather be more concerned about yourself to make sure you don't live in ignorance (darkness). If there is any area of your life, where you know you are not knowledgeable enough, start infusing yourself with knowledge in that area to make sure you don't live in ignorance (darkness) and under the manipulation of the devil.

GOD RULES THROUGH LIGHT

God indeed rules through light (knowledge). He is not a manipulator; neither does He force man to do anything against his wish. He is a God of knowledge and loves the knowledgeable. He can only relate with every individual based on their level of knowledge. This is the very reason why He sent his only begotten Son, into a world full of darkness to bring light to humanity because He loved man. It is now man's duty to either accept the light He has given to us or reject it. We can decide to live in light or darkness.

We can choose to live under the ruler-ship of God or under the ruler-ship of the devil. We can embrace knowledge or we can embrace ignorance. The choice is ours, yes the choice is yours. But let it be known to you though, that whichever choice you make determines if you will live a life of victory or a life of defect, a life of purpose or a life of pain, a life of suffering or a life of success. The choice is totally yours to make. I hope you make the right choice!

GOD IS HELPLESS IN OUR IGNORANCE

If God can only relate with us based on our level of knowledge that means God is limited to our ignorance. Ignorance actually limits God from intervening in the misfortunes of our personal lives and that of our society. Unbelievable! One might say. As unbelievable as it is, that is the truth. Believe it or not, it still will not change this truth.

Now as He drew near, He saw the city and wept over it, saying, if you had known, even you, especially in this your day, the things that make for your peace! But now they are

hidden from your eyes. For days will come upon you when your enemies will build an embankment around you, surround you and close you in on every side, and level you, and your children within you, to the ground; and they will not leave in you one stone upon another, because you did not know the time of your visitation.

Luke 19:41-44

The statements above are the words of Jesus Himself. The bible said He wept at the sight of their ignorance. He could not help them neither could He prevent this disaster from happening to them, because they were ignorant. Ignorance is indeed a strong limitation between us and God. God can only deliver us or intervene in the situations of our lives when we get knowledge of it. Without knowledge there can be no deliverance. You can now understand better, why the devil will do anything possible to hold you captive in ignorance.

In the first year of Darius the son of Ahasuerus, of the lineage of the Medes, who was made king over the realm of the Chaldeans in the first year of his reign I, Daniel, understood by the books the number of the years specified by the word of the Lord through Jeremiah the prophet, that He would accomplish seventy years in the desolations of Jerusalem. Then I set my face toward the Lord God to make request by prayer and supplications, with fasting, sackcloth, and ashes.

Daniel 9:1-3

Although Israel had completed their time (years) of being in slavery, yet deliverance did not come. WHY? Because of ignorance! There was no one who had knowledge as regards this. Not until Daniel discovered it. He, Daniel said "I understood by the books the number of years specified by the word of the Lord through Jeremiah the Prophet". Even though the numbers of the years were completed, they could not get their liberation, not until he had knowledge of this situation and began to pray, then and only then were they delivered. **KNOWLEDGE ALWAYS PRECEDES DELIVERANCE!**

This is to let us know how important knowledge is to our success, breakthrough, and deliverance as individuals and as a nation. GOD ONLY RULES IN LIGHT (Knowledge)! God rules and shines in Christ as Light Rules and generates Life by His Shining; God's Light Rules!

The Lord Jesus is the light of the world, and when He shines in us and on us, we will no longer walk in darkness but will have the light of life.

John 8:12

When God in Christ shines as the divine light, all darkness is eliminated, all rebellion and disorderliness is removed, and all lawlessness and resistance is exposed and dealt with. When God in Christ shines on us, there's a certain kind of ruling of light taking place – light rules, when God shines on us, His authority is installed in our being, the enemy is cast out, and anything of the darkness is exposed and removed.

When the divine light shines, all things are in oneness

and harmony, and as we live and walk in the light, we are being adjusted, brought back to where we should be, and kept in oneness and harmony with the saints and with everything and everyone around us. What keeps us in oneness and harmony is our habitual living under the ruling of the divine light. KNOWLEDGE!

If we say AMEN! To the divine light shining, exposing, infusing, and dispensing, we will spontaneously be one with the saints and we will live in harmony. But if we are in darkness and we don't come to the light, if we don't contact the Lord in His word in a living way and His light doesn't shine on us, we may think we are one and in harmony but we are actually in darkness, clueless about our situation and condition, and full of rebellion, resistance to God's will, lawlessness, and disorderliness.

However, when we come in the light, when we walk in the light and experience Christ as the light of life, all things in our being are in order and the divine life grows in us in a normal way. When the sun shines, everything is in order and life grows. When God in Christ shines in the New Jerusalem, the river of water of life proceeds from the throne of God and the tree of life grows on both its sides, producing twelve fruits, yielding its fruit each month! May we be the ones who habitually come to the light and live in the light so that we may be in oneness and harmony under the divine rule, and the divine life would grow in us in a normal way! In this way we have a foretaste of the New Jerusalem today!

LIGHT RULES WHEN IT SHINES

When there's darkness, there are all kinds of evil things happening, rebellion is there, and corruption is operating. But when the sun shines, everything is in the light, there is order, and life grows. When Christ came, in Him was life, and the life was the light of men (John 1:4). He told us that, if we follow Him as the light of the world, we will by no means walk in darkness but shall have the light of life (John 8:12). When the Lord shines on us again and again, the divine light controls and rules us.

The instability and disorderliness we have in Nigeria today and Africa at large is totally due to the absence of this light. The government is groping in darkness, the masses is groping in darkness, even believers that are meant to be the shining light has lost their shine due to ignorance. Then we complain of our nation's backwardness. We are the problem our nation has. We hold the solution to the problems of the African continent. We need to let our light shine.

When the brothers and sisters in Christ are regulated by the inward life growing in them and controlled by the divine light shining in them, the church life is kept in order, peace, oneness, and harmony. The reason there's no oneness and no harmony in the church is because the believers don't habitually walk in the light and they don't constantly allow God's light (knowledge) to shine in them. As seen in the New Jerusalem, in the church life today we have the invisible God in Christ shining with glory, and when He shines, all darkness is removed, all rebellion is terminated, and all disorderliness is set right. Light rules, and God in Christ on the throne shines and brings everyone under His authority by His shining.

Where there is darkness, there is chaos and confusion, but when light shines, things are set in order and the light rules and governs. In our Christian life and church life, we need to have God shining in us as light, and we will be brought under His authority. The church life is a miniature of the New Jerusalem, and so if we have God in Christ as the center, we will have light and everything will be under God's rule, kept in order, and we will be in oneness and harmony (see Gen. 1:3, 14-18; John 8:12; Eph. 1:10).

We can see this in Genesis 1 – when God restored and further created, He firstly restored light, and darkness was divided from light (see Gen. 1:3-16). The more light there is; the more separation and rule there is. When light shines, there is no confusion and no rebellion. When light shines, God is on the throne, Satan is subdued, darkness is eliminated, and all rebellion is cast out. When light shines, everything is kept in order under the rule of light.

LIGHT GENERATES LIFE AND CAUSES LIFE TO GROW

When the sun shines, the first thing that happens is that it rules and brings in order, and then all the living things can grow in life in a normal way. When God as light shines, firstly we are brought under the rule of God and then life is generated and life grows.

Life comes from light: if we are under God's shining light, life will be generated and the divine life will grow in us. In Genesis 1 we see that when light was restored, everything was in order under the rule of light, and then as a higher light was restored (the sun and the moon), life was generated. The higher the light the higher the life! In the New Jerusalem there will be the highest light –

God Himself as light shining through Christ, the Lamb-lamp, therefore there will be the highest life growing. As God shines in Christ, the river of life is flowing and the tree of life is growing and bearing fruit.

Christ came as light, and the life in Him was the light of the world; also, He came so that we may have life and may have it abundantly (John 10:10). Christ didn't come merely as light to shine on us and expose us; He came to shine on us, bring under God's rule by bringing us under His shining, and then generate life in us and cause the divine life to grow in us. From God as light, all the riches of life came forth. God in Christ is light, and from Him flows the river of water of life, in whose living water grows the tree of life (see 1 John 1:5; Rev. 22:1-2). This is so wonderful!

Where there is light, there's order, generating power and giving birth to. When God's shining light is accepted and welcomed in us, we will be set in order, all things will be in oneness and in harmony, and life will grow in a normal way. Then we can take the light into our society to bring an end to darkness through the shining of the light in us. "Christ in you the hope of glory". That we may have such a foretaste of the wonderful effects of God's shining light in the New Jerusalem today in the church, in our nation, continent and the world at large through imposing the values of the kingdom on earth and embracing light. LIGHT RULES! LIGHT BREEDS LIFE! LIGHT EMPOWERS!

NUGGETS
FROM CHAPTER 12

1. Light rules over darkness.
2. God can only relate with us based on our level of knowledge.
3. God is limited by our ignorance.
4. Ignorance is what is destroying us and not the devil.
5. The only power the devil has is in our area of ignorance.
6. God is helpless in our area of ignorance.
7. Ignorance is darkness.
8. Light generates life and causes it to grow.
9. When you live in light, you live under God's ruler-ship.
10. When you live in darkness, you live under the ruler-ship of the devil.

CHAPTER 13
....
CONSEQUENCES OF LACK OF KNOWLEDGE

"It is a common sentence that Knowledge is power; but who hath duly considered or set forth the power of Ignorance? Knowledge slowly builds up what Ignorance in an hour pulls down. Knowledge, through patient and frugal centuries, enlarges discovery and makes record of it; Ignorance, wanting its day's dinner, lights a fire with the record, and gives a flavor to its one roast with the burnt souls of many generations." (George Eliot)

My people are destroyed for lack of knowledge.

Hosea 4:6a

There are several grave consequences that come with lack of knowledge. The paramount is destruction. God Himself said in Hosea 4:6a "my people are destroyed for lack of knowledge". What a strong statement! My people are destroyed for lack of knowledge. This is rather amazing as a lot of us associate the destruction in different areas of our lives to different things except our ignorance.

God did not say what destroys His people is the devil,

He did not say it is the economy; He did not say it is our friends, relatives, family or neighbors as we often like to believe. But rather, He said the one thing destroying my people is lack of Knowledge.

How many times in our lives have we pushed the responsibilities for the failures in our lives to someone, or something else? It is high time we begin to take responsibilities of the happenings in our lives. Because whatever result or success you have in life is directly proportional to your level of knowledge. Knowledge acted upon makes all the difference, produces the different results we have in life. It means that the lack of knowledge is the foundation for all life failures, destruction, depression, difficulties, hatred, bitterness, envy, etc.

There are various cases that have shown or practically proven how inadequate knowledge or lack of knowledge is costly and deadly to individuals and the society at large. This is the very reason why this mountain of ignorance must be pulled down in our individual lives and the society at large. Individuals with superficial knowledge of a topic or subject may be worse off than people who know absolutely nothing. As Charles Darwin observed, "ignorance more frequently begets confidence than knowledge."

A case of interest is that of Mr. Rufus, he was a wealthy man worth millions of US dollars. He signed an undertaking with the bank for his friend to loan a huge amount of money. His friend promised to pay back in due season, that he wanted to invest in a huge business that would yield them three folds of the money they were lending. Mr. Rufus without adequate knowledge of the kind of business his friend was talking about, not seeking proper

248 ■ The Mountain Of Ignorance

knowledge of the risk that might be involved, decided to ignorantly sign this paper for his friend. Due to the huge promises the friend had made to him about the returns from the investment of which he would have 50 percent of the total interest.

Motivated by huge returns Mr. Rufus signed the papers for the loaning of money for his friend as his guarantor. Unfortunately, the business failed and the bank seized everything that belonged to Mr. Rufus, including his house. He became bankrupt and homeless. Receiving this news, Mr. Rufus developed heart attack that eventually led to his death. The grave consequences of one act of ignorance led to the untimely death of this gentle man that was doing well before his ignorant act. Friends, never underestimate the power of the consequences of ignorance.

Why must ignorance be destroyed? It must be destroyed because ignorance is the number one destroyer of the people of God. "My people are destroyed for lack of knowledge". There is no other force destroying us like ignorance. Ignorance is a limiting force, worst of all a force of destruction.

> *"Because there is no greater evil than ignorance and the destruction of genius. Ignorance has been responsible for more death, more bigotry, and more sin than any other force. It is the destroyer of mankind." (Richelle Mead)*

It is therefore of great importance and value, that we put an end to this Mountain. THE MOUNTAIN OF IGNORANCE must be leveled in order for us to efficiently accomplish our purpose on the earth and have a fulfilling life. This was one of the very first problems Jesus addressed in His ministry on earth. Jesus came to eradicate the problem of ignorance. He declared Himself as the light of the world. Most of the time when we talk about Jesus as I said earlier, we talk about Him only as the Savior of the world, but before He died to save the world, He had a ministry and that ministry was about eliminating ignorance (darkness) and all its consequences of destructions, calamities and sorrows in the world.

"Of all destructive forces in this world perhaps, known greater exist than sincere ignorance."
(Kelvin Bache)

This is the very ministry Jesus expects us to be doing on the earth today. But unfortunately we seem to have forgotten this part of the gospel, which is also as a result of our ignorance. And this has led to different kinds of destructions in our world today:

- Destruction in values
- Destruction in systems
- Destruction in our educational sector
- Destruction in our economy
- Destruction in marriages
- Destruction in families
- Destruction in our medical sector
- Destruction in our youths etc.

It's like we are having a harvest of destruction in our nations, continent and world today, all because of ignorance; THE MOUNTAIN OF IGNORANCE, for us to have a sane society today, we must bring down this mountain of ignorance in our society. Knowledge must be made available to every facet of the society, to everyone from the lowest to the highest.

We must eradicate ignorance and illiteracy from our nations and continent to the nearest minimum for us to have a national development. Illiteracy breeds more ignorance than you can ever begin to imagine. Ignorance can stifle learning, especially if the ignorant person believes that he or she is not ignorant. A person who falsely believes he or she is knowledgeable will not seek out clarification of his or her beliefs, but rather rely on his or her ignorant position. He or she may also reject valid but contrary information, neither realizing its importance nor understanding it. This concept is elucidated in Justin Kruger's and David Dunning's work, "Unskilled and Unaware of It: How Difficulties in Recognizing One's Own Incompetence Lead to Inflated Self-Assessments," otherwise known as the Dunning–Kruger effect.

The Dunning–Kruger effect is a cognitive bias wherein relatively unskilled individuals suffer from illusory superiority, mistakenly assessing their ability to be much higher than is accurate. The bias was first experimentally observed by David Dunning and Justin Kruger of Cornell University in 1999. Dunning and Kruger attributed the bias to the metacognitive inability of the unskilled to evaluate their own ability level accurately. Their research also suggests that conversely, highly skilled individuals may underestimate their relative competence, erroneously assuming that tasks that are easy for them are also easy for others.

Dunning and Kruger have postulated that the effect is the result of internal illusion in the unskilled and external misperception in the skilled: "The miscalibration of the incompetent stems from an error about the self, whereas the miscalibration of the highly competent stems from an error about others."

CONSEQUENCES OF ILLITERACY

The consequences of illiteracy are many and harmful in several respects. As well as affecting illiterate individuals themselves in their daily lives and often jeopardizing their future, this scourge has a significant effect on society, both socially and economically. The consequences of illiteracy on individuals and society include the following:

For individuals:

1. Limited ability to obtain and understand essential information.
2. Unemployment: The unemployment rate is 2–4 times higher among those with little schooling than among those with Bachelor's degrees.
3. Lower income; Lower-quality jobs.
4. Reduced access to lifelong learning and professional development.
5. Precarious financial position.
6. Little value is given to education and reading within the family, and this often leads to intergenerational transmission of illiteracy.
7. Low self-esteem, which can lead to isolation.
8. Impact on health: Illiterate individuals have

more workplace accidents, take longer to recover and more often misuse medication through ignorance of health care resources and because they have trouble reading and under-standing the relevant information (warnings, dosage, contraindications, etc.).

For society:

1. Since literacy is an essential tool for individ-uals and states to be compet-itive in the new global knowledge economy, many positions remain va-cant for lack of adequate trained personnel to hold them.

2. The higher the proportion of adults with low literacy proficiency is, the slower the overall long-term GDP growth rate is.

3. The difficulty understanding societal issues lowers the level of community involvement and civic participation.

4. Without the basic tools necessary for achieving their goals, individuals without an adequate level of literacy cannot be involved fully and on a completely equal basis in social and political discourse.

PERSONAL IGNORANCE LEADS TO SOCIETAL DESTRUCTION

We have to infuse knowledge into our society, making it available to every individual; that is the only way we can prevent personal ignorance from causing national disasters. If we concentrate on only ourselves, developing ourselves and ignoring the masses, sooner or later the ignorance of the masses will catch up with the nation and it will therefore affect you no matter how developed and knowledgeable you think you are.

We have to make it a personal responsibility to eradicate ignorance from our society. We should create different movements, NGO's for this purpose let us pull down this mountain.

I was told of a man who was sick mentally, instead of the man to be taken to a psychiatric hospital the family decided to take this man to a mountain for deliverance, as they believed that the reason for the sickness was the devil. On this mountain, the mentally sick man was denied food and being flogged everyday all in the name of flogging the devil out of him and starving the devil to death. Can you begin to imagine this level of ignorance?

What is even sadder about this story is that whatever they were doing they were doing it in the name of God. And the prophet they took this man to is supposed to be a Christian. Needless to say that within weeks this mentally sick man was dead out of the starvation leaving five children behind without anybody to train or make provisions for them. These children went into the streets to look for daily living, this was how they became hooligans on the street and a treat to the whole society at large.

You can see how, the ignorance of one person can cause a societal unrest. So we must not be nonchalant to the happenings around us if we want to live in a peaceful society and a prosperous nation. We must learn to speak against the evils in the society irrespective of who is practicing it, it has to stop.

NUGGETS
FROM CHAPTER 13

1. Ignorance leads to destruction.
2. Limitations in life are caused by ignorance.
3. It is like we are having a harvest of destruction in our society due to igno-rance.
4. We must all raise war against ignorance.
5. Ignorance leads to leaving in self-deception.
6. Personal ignorance leads to a negative impact on the society.
7. Ignorance leads to economic failures.
8. Ignorance leads to low income.
9. Illiteracy breeds more ignorance than you can ever imagine.
10. Ignorance can stifle learning, especially if the ignorant person believes that he or she is not ignorant.

CHAPTER 14

GOD ABHORS THE IGNORANT

> ....Because thou hast rejected knowledge, I will also reject thee, that thou shalt be no priest to me: seeing thou hast forgotten the law of thy God, I will also forget thy children.
>
> *Hosea 4:6b*

This scripture is a very popular scripture we often quote but I wonder how many people have really taken their time to analyze this scripture. This scripture explains perfectly well God's stand on ignorance.

> My people are destroyed for lack of knowledge. Because you have rejected knowledge, I also will reject you from being priest for Me; because you have forgotten the law of your God, I also will forget your children.
>
> *Hosea 4:6*

This is God actually speaking; He started by saying my people are destroyed for lack of knowledge. God saw the destruction coming the way of His people due to ignorance, yet He could not do anything about it, because He has given man the freedom of choice, the right to choice and free will, so He cannot go against His rule. This is to establish the fact that God will not help us in our area of ignorance; He is limited and helpless by our ignorance. God can only relate with us based on our level of ignorance.

God calls ignorance the rejection of knowledge, which simply means it is actually a choice to be ignorant. When you decide not to discipline yourself to seek for knowledge in any area, God sees it as the rejection of Knowledge.

The rejection of knowledge (ignorance) attracts a reaction from God. He said because you have rejected knowledge, I will also reject you from being priest to me. Wow! That is strong! I will reject you from being priest for me. God has no tolerance for ignorance; therefore we should not have tolerance for ignorance also. You can begin to imagine the weight of ignorance in the life of individuals.

God is not rejecting them from being priest for Him because they committed a sin. When they even commit sin, He said if you will only repent I will forgive you, but when it comes to Ignorance (rejection of knowledge) He said "I will reject you from being priest for me". God has zero percent tolerance to ignorance. He abhors the ignorant! If God so much detests Ignorance, then we should not make ignorance our companion, neither should we live in ignorance as our comfort zone. God knows the strong destructive force ignorance has on an individual and therefore cannot afford to allow a person who as a result of his/her ignorance is like an agent of destruction to himself and the society to represent Him.

> *"An ignorant person is, by the very fact of his or her ignorance, a very dangerous person."*
> *(Hendrik W. Van Loon)*

God is very particular about the issue of ignorance. Even though He is a loving God who loves all His children, yet He will not allow an ignorant person to represent Him. That does not mean He hates them, but ignorance is a disqualification for working with God. God has no regards for an ignorant person. Therefore if we really want to represent God in our day and time, we must embrace knowledge. You must make the seeking of knowledge your number one priority. Paul said to Timothy to study to show himself approved to God, a workman that need not to be put to shame.

Study to shew thyself approved unto God, a workman that needeth not to be ashamed, rightly dividing the word of truth.

2 Timothy 2:15

This is to let you know how important knowledge is to God. Paul's advice to Timothy was study, to show yourself approved to God. In other words pursue knowledge, acquire knowledge, get rid of ignorance in your life as a proof to God that you can be a priest for Him, or to qualify to be a priest for God. Your level of knowledge determines if you can be a priest for God or not. That is what stands as a yard stick for God accepting you or rejecting you.

God himself said it in the scripture above, that I will reject you from being priest to me. Not just that, but He will also forget your children because you have forgotten the law of your God. Can you imagine that? Can we say this is the reason why the church is irrelevant in the society today? Has God abandoned us for lack of knowledge?

Well I will leave you to answer that question. But if the church must be relevant today, the 21st century church must seek knowledge just the same way a starving man seeks for food.

It is only in Africa, especially Nigeria that churches encourage members to be lazy. How can a pastor organize meetings from Monday to Sunday for members expecting them to be in church and telling them it is their service to God? When people are supposed to be working they are milking them in the church and telling them to believe God for a miracle.

I was dumbfounded when I heard of a pastor that called for an urgent meeting on a Tuesday afternoon. He asked the messages should be sent to the church members that it was compulsory for every worker to be in attendance. One of the workers was a medical doctor and was on duty that particular day. When they send the information to him, he told them that he could not come as he was on duty and had patient to attend to. The pastor went into rage and issue and order that they should ask him to appear at the church immediately or face the consequences. As they have succeed in brain washing their members that if you do not do what your pastor says, you will be out of his covering.

However this doctor could not leave his patient unconscious in the emergency ward to obey dictators (pastors) order. So he stayed back to take care of the patient. The Sunday at church the pastor asked this young man to stand up and he gave him the disgrace of his life cursing him and saying that he will never go far in life because he did not obey the man of God. He never allowed this young man any opportunity to explain himself. After several minutes of verbal attack on this young man non-stop, the young man walked out never to return to the church again and they labeled him in the church as a rebel and backslider.

I cannot but ask myself where this preaches got these practices from, what bible they read and if Christ is still their role model. I am even more amazed at the gullible multitudes that follow these people. What level of ignorance, manipulation and stupidity? It is high time you embrace knowledge and begin to question anything you are being taught that has no biblical backing. Until will embrace knowledge the church in the 21st century will still be backward.

NUGGETS
FROM CHAPTER 14

1. God hates ignorance.
2. Lack of knowledge leads to rejection by God.
3. God cannot help you in your ignorance.
4. The number one price of ignorance is destruction.
5. Study to show yourself qualified for God's use.
6. Your level of knowledge will determine the level at which God relates with you.
7. When you reject knowledge, God rejects you.
8. To be relevant you must seek knowledge.
9. God has no regard for the ignorant.
10. Ignorance is a limitation.

CHAPTER 15

LET THE REVOLUTION AGAINST IGNORANCE BEGIN

"Ignorance is a virus. Once it starts spreading, it can only be cured by reason. For the sake of humanity, we must be that cure."
(Neil de Grasse Tyson)

You are welcome to the last chapter of this book, the chapter of solutions. From all the previous parts and chapters, we have been able to see the different types of ignorance, the dangers of ignorance to an individual and the society at large, limiting and destructive force of ignorance. In this chapter I will like to discuss with us how to put an end to ignorance in our individual lives and in our society. Stay with me, let's enjoy this ride together.

It is a common fact that ignorance is the absence of knowledge. Our number one goal therefore in our battle against ignorance should be how best we can get educative information across to everyone in the society, from the lowest to the highest. Building a system that will allow all vital information accessible to every citizen free of charge. So irrespective of the social status of the individual, everyone will have equal access to all vital and educative information.

262 ■ The Mountain Of Ignorance

FIGHT AGAINST ILLITERACY

Illiteracy is simply the inability to read and write. It is amazing that in this 21st century there are still a lot of people who cannot read and write in our world, especially in the continent of Africa. Illiteracy is the number one promoter of ignorance. so we have to put an end to illiteracy by building more schools, adult schools, promoting free education, where people could be taught the very primary basics, how to read and write. If you cannot read and write, there is no way you will escape living in ignorance. So the first step is putting an end to illiteracy among the common masses.

Fighting illiteracy today is not going to stop at teaching people how to read and write. The masses must be taught how to use computers, how to surf the Internet etc. I was amazed to discover that a huge amount of people do not know how to operate computers or use the Internet. Special centers should be built by the government and individuals where the masses can come to get free computer and Internet trainings. Computers should be made available in all our schools for students use.

The building of libraries should be a major project for all our villages, towns, cities, states and nations. We must cultivate the importance of the libraries into all our children. Students should be encouraged to study, do research and source for information as much as possible using the various libraries made available.

We must cultivate in our continent the culture of libraries, especially community libraries. Libraries and the idea of books must become part of our structure. We should not say this is not a typical African culture. Yes, that is true. We never used to have books in Africa.

We depended mainly on stories, tales and folklores. As much as we need to keep our culture, common sense also tells us that we must likewise aspire for progress. If library is a factor in civilization and development we have to embrace the idea.

You will be shocked to realize that even Europe never used to have a culture of libraries until the age of renaissance and enlightenment, when the desire for growth and progress became the aspiration and pursuit of the continent. They had to introduce libraries as a necessity for growth and development. We too can do the same thing.

> *"Without the library, you have no civilization."* (Ray Bradbury)

Europe at a point in her development also depended on tales, stories and folklores, but reality tells us that stories could be forgotten, tales and folklores could become buried in history, but books live forever. So I don't buy into the argument that libraries are not meant for Africans, because Africans naturally don't read. Yes, that was in our past.

We must only embrace the part of our past that is beneficial today and let go of the past that is holding us back. Let us replace the part of our culture that does not enhance our growth and development with other practices, better practices that have worked for other nations and continents. I would therefore rather advocate for libraries. We need them. Africa cannot afford to do without libraries; we would need another thousand years to experience development and true civilization. But with libraries, we can do it in a few decades.

"Without libraries what have we? We have no
past and no future." (Ray Bradbury)

Let me now give you the advantages of having the concept of libraries as part and parcel of our culture. We must know why libraries especially community libraries must be popularized in our nations and continent as a whole. Every village must have a library, every town must have a library, every home must have a library, every institution must have a library, every school must have a library, every mosque must have a library, every church must have a library, etc. Libraries must be the order of the day, it does not matter if it is going to be old school book based libraries or ultra-modern digital electronic libraries, but libraries must be embraced and celebrated in our continent.

"A library outranks any other one thing
a community can do to benefit its people.
It is a never failing spring in the desert."
(Andrew Carnegie)

Libraries as a Factor of Development, Knowledge and Civilization:

• Libraries help revitalize neighborhoods and downtowns.

• If we build attractive functional and community oriented libraries, we will bring life and development to our villages and neighborhoods.

• Through libraries, we could create a modern variant of cultural centers. Where apart from reading, foundations could be laid for interactions, relationships and creation of economic opportunities for the community.

- Libraries could become a major player in communities, towns, villages and cities. They could become agencies that the government and community would use to bring sustainability to the neighborhoods. Through it, we could develop the culture of resilience, self-reliance and sharing within the communities.

- Libraries could become a center from where specific community needs could be met. Poor families, pupils, students, could actually have their educational needs for text books, school works, met through community libraries.

- Libraries could be used as centers for preservation of history in forms of artifacts, digital and oral history, folklores, stories, audio recordings, etc.

- Through libraries, communities and townships could come to know themselves better, their history, their heroes, etc.

- Libraries could become a catalyst for resolving social problems for the township, communities, and neighborhood.

- We could use libraries to disseminate the right value system all over the nation. Values of democracy, freedom, justice could be promoted through libraries. Sometimes in bigger cities, we need to have special buildings for libraries. Thereby libraries become a source of economic stimulation by creating employment, jobs and other economic activities around the libraries.

- Libraries could become a center of motivation for small and middle scale businesses. That way, the spirit of enterprise and entrepreneur-ship could be developed.

With these listed points, I believe you will agree with me that with establishment of libraries, we will be able to reduce common ignorance to the nearest minimum.

THE ROLE OF THE CHURCH

The church must begin to teach sound doctrines on her pulpit. Bringing down all superstitions and false doctrines, the dignity of labor must be taught in our churches and the beauty of hard work must be appreciated. The people should be trained and released back into the society to bring the light of the kingdom into the different spheres of the nation, thereby pulling down THE MOUNTAIN OF IGNORANCE!

Different NGO's, movements, organizations should be raised by the church to address the different areas of ignorance in the society. The Church should be involved in major projects for the society. Like building education centers, libraries, computer centers etc.

PERSONAL RESPONSIBILITY

Every individual should be taught to take personal responsibility for self-development, acquisition of knowledge, studies and eradicating ignorance from their personal lives. On personal notes, everyone should be involved in enlightening the masses on every scale within their reach as much as possible. We shouldn't close our eyes to the ignorance of individuals in our families, neighborhoods, environment, villages, cities, states, nations, continents and our world at large.

WAR AGAINST IGNORANCE

We must come together as a nation, to join force together to fight against ignorance, different organizations, NGO's, movements, rallies, camps, trainings, social clubs, interactive forums, groups, educative game programs etc. must be started for this cause.

We must be true ambassadors of Christ on the earth in order to be able to put an end to the plague of ignorance in our society. The mountain of ignorance must be pulled down. We have to seek knowledge, and infuse ourselves with so much light that can only come from knowledge. Then we can strategically infuse the society with this same light. Thereby eradicating darkness from our various societies and setting people free from the power of ignorance.

Believers must step out of the four walls of the church and take the gospel of the kingdom into every sphere of life. We have to bring our light to the society. For gross darkness has overshadowed the earth. It is in this gross darkness that our light will be relevant not in the four walls of the church but in our society. We have to go out and shine our light, the nation needs us the world needs us.

Arise, shine; for your light has come! And the glory of the Lord is risen upon you. For behold, the darkness shall cover the earth and deep darkness the people; But the Lord will arise over you, and His glory will be

seen upon you. The Gentiles shall come to your light, and kings to the brightness of your rising.

Isaiah 60:1-3

We must arise to shine, for darkness has covered the earth. Our responsibility is to shine. When we begin to shine, the darkness of ignorance will disappear from our society. You will agree with me that there is gross darkness in Nigeria and Africa at large. This darkness is the darkness caused by ignorance. It is time to step out to face the challenge, the giant of ignorance. Ignorance must be leveled in our society, so that we might have a breath of fresh air and live a happy and fulfilled life, knowing that we have fulfilled purpose. Darkness has no power over light, the victory is already ours, let's go out and shine to the glory of God. Nigeria and Africa will surely be great. Arise brethren! Arise church! Arise Pastors! Let the people Arise!

NUGGETS
FROM CHAPTER 15

1. Eradicating ignorance through the establishment of information centers.
2. Individuals should take personal responsibility for knowledge acquisition and campaigns against ignorance.
3. Fight against illiteracy.
4. Importance of libraries.
5. Introduction of computer literacy.
6. Making information easy and accessible to all.
7. The messages on our pulpit must change. We must put an end to super-stition in our churches.
8. The role of the Church in the eradication of ignorance.
9. It is our responsibility to enlighten our people.
10. Arise and shine!

CONCLUSION

The mountain of ignorance! Now that you have gone through the whole book, I believe that in this book, you have seen the root and source of all the pain, sorrow and tragedy that have befallen our continent. When we talk about Africa, most people think the reason for our tragedy is lack of money. I pray that this book will spread all over Africa, to every nook and cranny, towns and villages, so that people will know that the reason we are poor is because we are ignorant.

We are not poor because we do not have money, we are poor because we do not know how to make money. I pray that this book will get to the hands of pupils in primary, secondary and tertiary schools so that they will be able to take their lives into their hands instead of waiting for some spiritual power or forces to come and give them what they need in life. I pray that this book will deliver all those who are bond by the bondage of religion and false spirituality and all forms of superstition to be ready to confront the challenge of their age and build a better present and future for themselves and their children.

This book might be one of the most important books that has ever been written to set the people of Africa and other developing world free from all the deception that have been destroying them. No wonder our Lord God Himself says, that the only force of destruction in life is the force of ignorance, it is not Satan that destroys but ignorance. For my people are destroyed for lack of knowledge. God's people need to fight against ignorance, God's church need to declare war against ignorance.

The church needs to arise not just against total and absolute ignorance, the church also needs to arise against half-truth or falsehood, which is some of the things that are prevailing in our churches today. It is time for us the Africans especially the Nigerian church to arise and confront these things and speak the truth to liberate our people and nation and to build a better future for our continent. The next generation of Africans must be able to see a better continent, better life, better future and better destiny. If that is supposed to happen it will only happen thanks to the power of light, power of understanding and to the strength of knowledge.

So, I pray that this book will trigger that movement into liberation, the movement into freedom, the movement into deliverance from religious mental captivity. May the Lord bless you as you spread the word and let us arise and destroy this mountain that has reduced us to dwarfs. Let us arise and fight against these mountains that have turned us to blind men and women and a dark continent. Let us arise and pull down this mountain. Let us say like Caleb: give me this mountain and I will destroy it, I will turn it into flat land. Let the church of Africa arise like in the power of Caleb, in the strength of Joshua and throw the challenge to the mountain of ignorance, turning it into a flat ground in our generation. Thereby making our children to enjoy the beauty of the gospel of the kingdom of God. Let this mountain be removed, let this mountain be cast into the sea and let Africa and the world be free. In Jesus name AMEN!

Sunday Adelaja Bio

Sunday Adelaja is a Nigerian born Leader, Transformation Strategist, Pastor, and Innovator.

At 19, he won a scholarship to study in the former Soviet Union. He completed his master's program in Belorussia State University with distinction in journalism.

At 33, he had built the largest evangelical church in Europe; The Embassy of the Blessed Kingdom of God for All Nations.

Sunday Adelaja is one of the few individuals in our world who has been privileged to speak in the United Nations, Israeli Parliament, Japanese Parliament, and United States Senate.

The movement he pioneered has been instrumental in reshaping lives of people in the Ukraine, Russia and about 50 other nations where he has his branches.

His congregation, which consists of ninety-nine percent white Europeans, is a cross-cultural model of the church for the 21st century.

His life mission is to advance the Kingdom of God on earth by raising a generation of history makers who will live for a cause larger, bigger, and greater than themselves. Those who will live like Jesus and transform every sphere of the society in every nation as a model of the Kingdom of God on earth.

His economic empowerment program has succeeded in raising over 200 millionaires in the short period of three years.

Sunday Adelaja is the author of over 300 books; many of which are translated into several languages including Russian, English, French, Chinese, German, etc.

His work has been widely reported by world media outlets such as; The Washington Post, The Wall Street Journal, New York Times, Forbes, Associated Press, Reuters, CNN, BBC, German, Dutch and French national television stations.

Pastor Sunday is happily married to his "Princess" Bose Dere Adelaja. They are blessed with three children; Perez, Zoe and Pearl.

FOLLOW SUNDAY ADELAJA
ON SOCIAL MEDIA

Subscribe And Read Pastor Sunday's Blog:
www.sundayadelajablog.com

Follow These Links And Listen To Over 200 Of Pastor Sunday`s Messages Free Of Charge:
http://sundayadelajablog.com/content/

Follow Pastor Sunday on Twitter:
www.twitter.com/official_pastor

Join Pastor Sunday's Facebook page to stay in touch:
www.facebook.com/pastor.sunday.adelaja

Visit our websites for more information about Pastor Sunday's ministry:
http://www.godembassy.com
http://www.pastorsunday.com
http://sundayadelaja.de

CONTACT

For distribution or to order bulk copies of
this book,
please contact us:

USA
CORNERSTONE PUBLISHING
info@thecornerstonepublishers.com
+1 (516) 547-4999
www.thecornerstonepublishers.com

AFRICA
Sunday Adelaja Media Ltd.
Email: btawolana@hotmail.com
+2348187518530, +2348097721451,
+2348034093699.

LONDON, UK
Pastor Abraham Great
abrahamagreat@gmail.com
+447711399828, +44-1908538141

KIEV, UKRAINE
pa@godembassy.org
Mobile: +380674401958

BEST SELLING BOOKS BY DR. SUNDAY ADELAJA

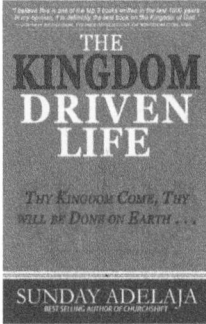

The Kingdom Driven Life:
Thy Kingdom Come, Thy
Will be Done on Earth
(Best seller)

Myles Munroe:
... Finding Answers To Why Good
People Die Tragic And Early Deaths

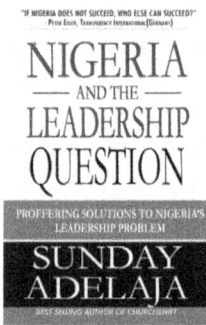

Nigeria And
The Leadership Question:
Proffering Solutions To Nige-
ria's Leadership Problem

Olorunwa (There Is Sunday):
Portrait Of Sunday Adelaja.
The Roads Of Life.

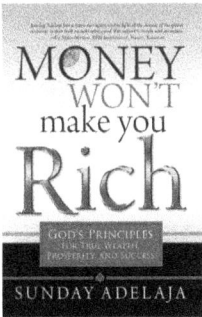

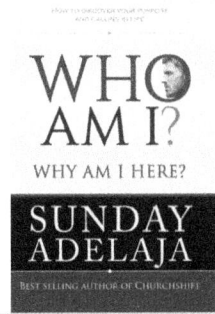

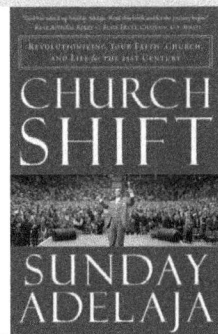

www.ingramcontent.com/pod-product-compliance
Lightning Source LLC
Chambersburg PA
CBHW022118080426
42734CB00006B/178